WHEN WILL I BE GOOD ENOUGH?

How to Overcome Low Self-Worth and
How to Find Happiness Again

SOPHIE DAWSON

TABLE OF CONTENTS

INTRODUCTION

At times we all have feelings of self-doubt and question if we are really good enough in a variety of situations throughout life. To an extent, this is human nature. Pushing ourselves that bit more allows the human race to question what we know, research, innovate and change, all of which help us to evolve. This is good and necessary. However, when we continuously question our abilities and allow self-doubt to take over it becomes counterproductive and harmful to us.

We believe that we can only be good enough, worthy enough human beings if we meet certain criteria. We define these criteria by what we observe from others, much of which is what we see in the media. What we see in the media is "perfection." Rarely do people post pictures of themselves at their worst. People like to display the best parts of their lives to give the illusion that life is rosy. If the media posts unflattering photos of celebrities, they highlight the flaws with unkind words and ridicule. In response, we pile pressure and stress on ourselves every day to "match" what we see, or what we think we are seeing or the expectations we believe to be upon us. We frantically try to tick off tasks on our endless daily to-do lists, create and meticulously maintain the perfect home, preen ourselves to try and look like the latest catwalk model, be seen to be practicing perfect parenting, have a highly paid career, and still have time to go to the spa before meeting friends for lunch.

Feeding these feelings of self-doubt is the fact that we live in a world where social media misguides our perception of others and where being "super busy" is the new norm, in fact, it is trendy, which means you need to jump on the busy bandwagon, or risk being left behind.

It's no wonder we begin to develop feelings of low self-worth when we make such unrealistic comparisons and increasingly pile on the pressure to achieve "everything." The problem is that we are programmed into thinking in this way by society. Society links being "busy" with being "productive" and tells us that the more productive we are, the higher our self-worth. The social pressure to strive for perfection and link our productivity to our self-worth is, in fact, harming our productivity. We are all in competition with one another to be the busiest and, therefore, the worthiest. We feel compelled to send late-night emails and work on the weekends to show we are worthy of our job. We take part in the "who had less sleep" competition and continuously remind ourselves and others that "there is never enough time," thus reinforcing our busy schedule. In actual fact, we have made ourselves so "busy" that we are no longer productive. Instead of being efficient, we are now running around with our hair on fire feeling totally exhausted and overwhelmed by the tireless stress of competing with our peers and it's all in vain. Stop the madness.

The truth is that nobody is really meeting all of these "criteria." However they may present themselves or be presented in the media, it's just not real life. However perfect someone's life may seem from the outside, you can bet your bottom dollar that they struggle with many of the same life challenges as we all do.

As human beings, we spend half our life sleeping and there is a very good reason for that—we need rest time in order for our bodies to function properly. Running ourselves ragged usually results in us just spinning our wheels to no avail.

The sad fact is that most of us suffer from feelings of low self-worth at some point or another in our lives. Perhaps we have just been made redundant and feel a blow to our self-confidence and a sickening uncertainty about our ability to bag another job to cover the bills. Maybe we invested heavily in something that didn't pay off or experienced a relationship breakup that sees us riding solo and feeling a bit lost. Sometimes we experience repeated or prolonged spells of low self-worth. Missing yet another promotion at work, battling with constant weight fluctuations or continuously falling short of our goals. These repeated or prolonged periods of low self-worth can cause us to question our capabilities and ask, "when will I be good enough?" The answer to which lies here, in this book.

By exploring the sociological, psychological, physical and emotional factors that influence how we perceive the world you can gain perspective, learn how to work smarter, not harder, positively change your mindset to boost self-worth and feel more content in daily life.

CHAPTER ONE

WHEN WILL I BE GOOD ENOUGH?

You flick onto social media for the fourth time that day and see an endless list of happy photos from acquaintances, friends from school, college, work, parenting groups, and other random people or others you have decided to follow based on their interests or perhaps your interest in them and their perfectly curated feed. As you scroll through these pictures and witness countless examples of fun family days out, work trips abroad, and adventurous holidays to far-off places, you begin to feel a sense of inferiority.

They all have so much to be proud of, you think to yourself. They own their own business, he's always jetting off on trips around the world, they are married with two beautiful children, she has another promotion, that couple has a huge house and two really expensive cars and I don't have any of those things, nor do I look as beautiful as any of them.

If their social media pages are anything to go by, they are wealthier, more successful, better looking, and far happier than you. You close the app again, feeling like a failure and wondering when it will be your turn to succeed. When you see everyone's perfect lives flaunted each day, you can't help thinking about how you compare. It seems as though you come up short in every area of your life. You aren't there enough for your children. You haven't reached the top rung of the ladder in your job and you never get the opportunity to travel. You don't work out at the gym enough. You aren't a very good partner, friend, or colleague. You aren't financially successful enough, you aren't skilled enough, talented enough, nice enough, or smart enough. All of these comparisons lead you to keep asking one question: When will I be good enough?

Being good enough is a yearning we've had since we were very young. Society is in part to blame for this obsession. Right from the day we begin school, we're supposed to meet certain expectations, and if we don't succeed we're made to feel like a failure. In contrast, those of our peers who manage to meet expectations are celebrated. The need to be good enough is fostered even earlier. As toddlers, there are a number of developmental milestones we're expected to meet. According to the CDC,[1] by the age of six months, a baby is supposed to be able to sit up by itself. By one year of age, a baby should be able to stand by holding onto something. These developmental milestones are set up to help identify developmental delays. The problem is that most parents take them far too seriously. If their child doesn't naturally meet these milestones, parents can tend to panic and begin to push their children before they're ready. Comparisons with other children increase the parent's anxiety and they become fixated on

---

[1] "CDC's Developmental Milestones | CDC."
https://www.cdc.gov/ncbddd/actearly/milestones/index.html. Accessed 20 Jun. 2021.

making their child walk by a certain age or become toilet-trained when they are expected. For the child, this means they are taught from a very early age that their parent's praise is associated with meeting certain behavioral criteria. If they don't meet these criteria, the child may begin to feel like they've failed to win their parent's acceptance.

According to psychologist Erik Erikson,[2] children between the ages of 6 and 11 begin to make comparisons with their peers. Realizing their efforts do not result in the same positive outcome as their peers, these children begin to feel incompetent. Moving on to the teenage years, these children begin to notice that the adults in their life don't praise them as readily as they used to. This is because now that the teens are older more is expected of them. It's at this time that young teens begin to take note of disappointment from the adults in their life. If this disapproval comes from someone they care about, the likelihood is that it will have a significant effect on their self-esteem.

The way most school systems are structured can set some pupils up to fail. The more a student fails, the less likely they are to engage in learning. In one survey at the University of Capetown,[3] fear of failure led to procrastination and avoidance. In other words, once a child starts to have bad grades, they are no longer likely to study or learn due to fear of failure. What this means is that bad performance at

---

[2] "Causes of Low Self Esteem in Kids - Verywell Family." 16 Nov. 2020, https://www.verywellfamily.com/causes-of-low-self-esteem-in-kids-3288009. Accessed 20 Jun. 2021.

[3] "The Fear Factor - Journal of Information Technology Education." https://www.jite.org/documents/Vol9/JITEv9p147-171Rogerson803.pdf. Accessed 20 Jun. 2021.

school leads to further decreased performance which in turn can lead to low self-esteem.

It's easy to see how early developmental hiccups can eventually lead to low self-esteem in teens. The toddler who perceives disappointment from their parents over developmental milestones might enter the school system with a sensitivity toward and a need for adult approval. They would likely be more sensitive to failure within the school system and be more likely to develop low self-esteem as a result.

Childhood is when we figure out our place in the world. The time in development when we gain self-awareness and start comparing ourselves with others is crucial for developing self-esteem. It is the low self-esteem that we develop as children that determines how we feel about ourselves as adults. The feeling of not being good enough stems from these small moments in our childhood where we learned we didn't quite cut it.

So, if we learn our place in the world during childhood, and if our self-esteem is established during this period, is there anything we can do to make ourselves feel good enough by the time we're an adult? The answer is yes, absolutely. Your brain is not hardwired. Even by the time we're fully grown, we can change the way we think. The longer we've behaved a certain way, the more difficult it is to change the way we think, but we can change. *You* can change. You can undo what you thought you knew about yourself when you were a child, a teenager, and even now as an adult.

Please note, at this point, you might be feeling emotional. This is perfectly normal. Feeling like you will never be good enough is not nice. Such feelings are often repressed and when they're brought to the surface, the truth of how bad it makes you feel can hit hard. Take a breath if you find this difficult. Be kind to yourself and let yourself feel whatever emotions come over you and know that you will be offered all of the tools you will need to help you learn how to feel like you *are* good enough.

CHAPTER SUMMARY

- Comparing yourself to others leads you to wonder if you're good enough.
- We have strived to be good enough since childhood when we were rewarded for milestones like becoming toilet-trained.
- When students fail at school they can develop low self-esteem, which contributes to a low sense of self-worth.
- Some experiences we go through when we are young can make us feel bad about ourselves. We can undo the damage done to our sense of self-worth when we become adults.

In the next chapter, you will learn....

- How abuse, low attachment, adverse experiences, and trauma can lead to having a low sense of self-worth
- How being from a minority and low socio-economic groups can lead to having a low sense of self-worth
- About how beauty standards, social media, mood disorders, and some physical issues can contribute to feeling worthless.

CHAPTER TWO

CAUSES OF LOW SELF-WORTH

Self-worth is our sense of how worthy we are as a person. Unlike self-confidence and self-esteem, self-worth is not based on what you do or how confident you are. It's about *who* you are and whether you feel you are valuable as a person.

Many of the things we experience can disrupt the development of a healthy sense of self-worth. It may be hard for you to pinpoint the cause of your own feeling of low self-worth. Some of the things that cause a sense of low self-worth are listed below. Don't feel bad if none of these things seem to relate to you. You may not remember what happened to make you feel the way you do. The important thing to understand is that it's not your fault. You aren't simply unworthy. Something has made you feel that way and we're going to help you change your way of thinking.

ABUSE

Of all the sources of childhood trauma, childhood abuse has the biggest negative effect on feelings of self-worth. When a child is sexually or physically abused they tend to blame themselves for what has happened to them. Children soon learn to associate punishment with bad behavior. They know that if they do something wrong, they'll get punished for it. So, when an adult subjects them to physical, sexual, or psychological abuse, experience tells them they must have done something to deserve it. In other words, abused children learn to blame themselves for the abuse they've suffered. In trying to understand what they've done to deserve this punishment children are left with only one conclusion: that they deserve to be abused because they aren't worthy of respect or kindness. Considering that victims of childhood abuse have done nothing to deserve the punishment they've received it's easy to see why they turn the blame on themselves. This feeling of blame will follow abuse victims into adulthood. The shame and incompetence that survivors of abuse feel in adulthood contribute to a low sense of self-worth. Even if an adult survivor comes to know on a logical level that the abuse was not their fault, subconsciously they may not be able to let go of the blame easily.

ATTACHMENT ISSUES

In attachment theory, it is suggested that in order to experience healthy relationships as an adult, children must make positive attachments with caregivers during childhood. Poorly attached children aren't given a sense of trust that their caregiver/s will be there for them and accept them for who they are. This leads to poor relationships in adulthood as well as a low sense of self-worth. There are many other causes of low attachment in children, such as having an absent parent. A child will not form a close attachment with a parent who is psychologically or emotionally absent. The parent who spends most of their time at work and who misses milestones and important moments in their child's life is not doing enough to form an attachment with their child. Sometimes overattachment can also lead to a low sense of self-worth. Parents who are overbearing or who don't allow their children any independence can lead to a child being overly attached. If a child doesn't develop a strong sense of independence they can become overly reliant on a parent. Overly attached children can be overpraised. Overpraising can lead to disappointment when the child enters school. They suddenly realize they aren't as good at everything as their parents led them to believe. This can lead to a huge blow to their self-esteem and eventually culminate in having a low sense of self-worth because they can't ever live up to the idea their parent, or parents, had of them.

ADVERSE EXPERIENCES OR TRAUMA

Our sense of power over our lives can be disrupted by adverse experiences or trauma. The death of a loved one, parental abandonment, parents divorcing, being bullied, losing a home, loss of income, illness, growing up in poverty, having an alcoholic parent, or anything that makes us question our sense of self are all experiences that can make us feel powerless. Where once we felt in control of our environments, our safety, and our judgment, after the trauma we may feel out of control. If something bad happens it's hard not to blame ourselves. We might wonder if there was something we might have done to prevent the trauma from happening. For instance, if we were quicker thinking, stronger, more intelligent, or if we'd been better in some way, the bad outcome might've been avoided. If we lost a loved one in an accident, such as a bad fall or a car crash, we might blame ourselves in some way for not being able to save them. We might think that being bullied is caused by our being unlikable, strange, or ugly. If our parents divorced, we might think it's because we drove them apart or that they didn't love us enough to stay together. Blaming yourself for the negative things that happen to you can lead to feeling unworthy.

MINORITY GROUPS

Being viewed as different can put people from minority groups at greater risk of being treated differently. People from minority groups will often have a low sense of self-worth due to experiencing bullying, racism and discrimination.

Unfriendliness and even hostility from people toward neurodiverse people led to a low sense of self-worth in participants of one study.[4] For 83% of participants, the main challenge faced by neurodiverse people was the lack of acceptance and understanding of their neurodiversity. Neurodiverse individuals also tend to be less successful in gaining employment and housing. All of these things add to the general feeling of low self-worth among people with neurodiversity.

---

[4] "Neurodiversity, Quality of Life, and Autistic Adults: Shifting Research ...." https://dsq-sds.org/article/view/1069/1234. Accessed 21 Jun. 2021.

For minority groups, racism can lead to low self-esteem, according to one study.[5] The sense of shame that results from racism against minorities can lead to a feeling of not belonging or not being accepted. The shame associated with not belonging is turned inward to the point where an individual's sense of self-worth is decreased.

SOCIO-ECONOMIC DIFFERENCES

The "scarcity effect" experienced by people who are in the low socio-economic group means they are more focused on the struggle of living day to day than anything else. The result of this is that they tend to have "negative self-stereotyping," according to one study.[6] Subjects reported feeling like they had low competence and that they felt like they were flawed due to being in the lower socio-economic group. This low sense of self-worth was driven by the opinions of others in society and portrayed in social media. Another study[7] showed that teachers were more likely to describe children in poverty as having negative traits simply because of their background. When children are treated differently because of their socio-economic status, they are likely to internalize these belief systems, leading to a low sense of self-worth. When society, their peers, teachers, and the media portray

[5] "Examining associations between racism, internalized shame, and ...." https://www.tandfonline.com/doi/full/10.1080/23311908.2020.1757857. Accessed 21 Jun. 2021.
[6] "How being poor can lead to a negative spiral of fear and self-loathing." https://www.theguardian.com/society/2015/jun/30/poverty-negative-spiral-fear-self-loathing. Accessed 23 Jun. 2021.
[7] "Children from poorer families perceived by teachers ... - The Guardian." 9 Jun. 2015, https://www.theguardian.com/education/2015/jun/09/teachers-poorer-children-education-primary-school. Accessed 23 Jun. 2021.

poorer people negatively, there is little chance for this group to have a healthy sense of their worth.

PHYSICAL CAUSES

One's own perception of our physical appearance can have a big effect on our sense of self-worth. The way you look can make you feel like you aren't worthy. So much emphasis is placed on beauty and physical perfection in the media that we as individuals can place too much importance on how we look. Better-looking people are said to be treated differently by others. People who are perceived as good-looking are more likely to be popular at school. They are more likely to be successful in gaining employment than people who are deemed as less attractive. It's even worse for people who are deemed unattractive. These people may be teased or laughed at during childhood. The shame and hurt from teasing may have lifelong effects on an individual's perception of themselves. They may feel unworthy as a person simply because of the way they look. People who are disabled can struggle with day-to-day activities. When they're young they definitely stand out from their peers. According to the Journal of Clinical Sports Psychology, people with disabilities tend to have a lower sense of self-esteem than able-bodied people. Stigmatization of disabled people was said to contribute to their having a low sense of self-worth. The ideal body, as seen in the media, is able-bodied. This lack of representation for disabled people can leave them feeling even more like outsiders making them feel even less worthy.

IMPOSSIBLE STANDARDS OF BEAUTY

The media has always placed undue emphasis on physical beauty. Since the advent of social media, beauty standards have put more pressure on people to reach unattainable standards of beauty. At one time only professional photographers working for top model agencies were regularly known to airbrush images. These days, with filters, apps, and a little photoshop know-how, everyday people have started to doctor their own images on social media. We are constantly bombarded with images of perfection. These "perfect" images have become so extreme that many represent bodies that are anatomically impossible. There have been a number of airbrushing scandals in which famous people or companies have been called out for posting images that are so airbrushed that they are physically impossible. For instance, L'Oreal[8] was forced to withdraw advertising that included highly airbrushed photos of celebrities. The problem with this extreme airbrushing is that normal bodily changes that go along with aging, such as weight gain, wrinkles, and sagging, are hidden from view. This means that people who start to experience these normal changes begin to feel like they are somehow aberrant. They may start to feel like aging is something to be ashamed of. Comparisons to celebrities, whose skin is as smooth in their forties and fifties as it was in their teens, are bound to leave people feeling inferior and even ashamed.

---

[8] "L'Oréal ads banned over 'airbrushing' | The Independent | The ...." 28 Oct. 2011, https://www.independent.co.uk/news/media/advertising/l-or-233-al-ads-banned-over-airbrushing-2326477.html. Accessed 23 Jun. 2021.

SOCIAL MEDIA

Not only does social media raise the standard of beauty unnaturally high, but it also makes people feel like they need to stand out in some way to be deemed worthy. Influencers need to be talented in some way, or they need to be entertaining, brilliant, beautiful, and exceptional to get attention. This may make some followers of social media feel inferior by comparison, especially if they themselves struggle to get any attention on these platforms. Although self-worth shouldn't relate to what people look like, what they can do, or how popular they are, social media makes these things seem more important than anything else. If you aren't attractive on social media, you had better be incredibly smart, have some extreme talent, or be incredibly funny or entertaining. Otherwise, it can feel like you don't matter and exacerbate feelings of worthlessness.

MOOD DISORDERS

Whatever the cause, mood disorders, like depression, can make it difficult to view the world with positivity. People with clinical depression are more likely to have a low sense of self-worth. In one study, many people with depression reported[9] not only feeling low in mood, but also feeling low about themselves. They described themselves as being inferior to friends and family members. They also had a negative view of themselves. Some didn't like themselves and others felt worthless. Some reported acting differently than the way

---

[9] "Depression and low mood (young people) - Depression, self and ...."
https://healthtalk.org/depression-and-low-mood/depression-self-and-self-esteem.
Accessed 25 Jun. 2021.

they felt by showing confidence outwardly when they felt worthless inside. It's hard to say whether low self-worth contributes to depression or whether depression leads to a low sense of self-worth. The two are closely related, as most questioned in this study described have a low sense of self-worth.

Note: Once more this discussion may bring out some emotions in you that you weren't aware of. You may have repressed some things from the past that have caused you to feel like you are unworthy. Just know you are taking the first steps to make yourself feel better, stronger, and more worthy. Hang in there! Give yourself a pat on the back. Facing the truth takes courage.

CHAPTER SUMMARY

- Children blame themselves when they are abused and shame leads to low self-worth as an adult.

- Not being well attached during childhood can lead to feeling worthless.

- Adverse experiences or trauma can lead to feelings of worthlessness.

- Minorities, people with physical issues, and those from lower socio-economic backgrounds can feel stigmatized, giving them a low sense of self-worth.

- Impossible beauty standards and perfect lives shown in social media can lead to feelings of inferiority.

- Mood disorders like depression can make people feel bad about themselves.

In the next chapter, you will learn....

- How some attempts to overcome your low sense of self-worth can make things worse.

- How comparing yourself to others and social media can make you feel even less worthy.

CHAPTER THREE

PITFALLS TO AVOID WHEN MANAGING LOW SELF-WORTH

We may deal with a low sense of self-worth in a number of ways that don't actually increase our self-worth and that may, in fact, lower it. Some of the ways we respond to having a low sense of self-worth might seem quite positive, such as seeking perfection or becoming an overachiever. You would think trying to be perfect would increase one's opinion of oneself. This is not the case when people have a low sense of self-worth.

OVERACHIEVING

One response to a feeling of low self-worth is to try to make up for feeling like a failure by becoming a high achiever. The problem with this response is that it doesn't get to the root of the problem. Having a low sense of self-worth means a person doesn't think they are worthy. As this is a deep-rooted belief that exists on a subconscious level, no matter how much a person tries to become an overachiever, they can never be good enough. If you don't treat the cause of low self-worth, then no amount of effort you put into achieving will make you feel like you matter.

SEEKING PERFECTION

People who have a low perception of their worth may make up for this by becoming perfectionists. Trying to do your best at something can be a good thing. It's when you become obsessed with being perfect that there's a problem. The problem with constantly striving for perfection is that you will never be happy with the result. You will always try to do better. You will never be able to reach perfection. Even if, for a moment, you feel good about an achievement or a task, the next time you attempt the same thing, you won't be happy with the same result. You will seek to do even better! This will put more pressure on you to achieve. Perfectionism can spill over into other parts of your life until almost everything you do has to be done perfectly in order to avoid the feeling of failure. This obsession for perfection can affect the people around you. Co-workers might become tired of you always setting the bar so high and making them look bad. Obsessive perfectionists often also expect the same level of perfectionism from family members and friends, which can put a strain on relationships. In the case of your children, you may be setting them up for having a low sense of self-worth. Your own low sense of self-worth may make you try to build up their success by pushing them. But you may end up pushing them too far, to the point where they don't think they're good enough.

BEING TOO BUSY

In an attempt to make up for feelings of low self-worth, some people try to make themselves busy, as if simply doing more will make them a better person. The trouble with this is that quantity does not always equal quality. Filling every minute of every day by running around doing as much as possible means that you won't be doing a good job at anything. Each task will only be half-done because you simply haven't got enough time to do everything you have planned. Being too busy can have consequences for your health. Everyone needs downtime. You need time to rest and recuperate. Filling your day up with too many tasks means you run the risk of burnout from lack of sleep and rest. You could develop high blood pressure and physical problems like acid reflux and stomach ulcers from constantly being under stress.

SETTING HIGH STANDARDS FOR OURSELVES

If you don't feel good about yourself, one of the ways to try to make yourself feel more worthy is to have high standards for your own success. High standards can be a good thing—if you can meet them. If we try to boost our own opinion of ourselves by setting standards so high that we struggle to achieve what we set out to do, then the opposite will occur. We will end up disappointed in ourselves for not being able to meet our own high standards. This can lead to us being overly critical of ourselves. We set ourselves up to fail by trying to do better than our skills, time or resources enable us to be. This makes us feel like we can't do anything right. Soon we can become critical of everything we do. Everyone has difficulty sometimes. Circumstances can get in the way of the tasks we're trying to achieve or the goals we've set. It's important to be flexible and prepared for when life throws us the odd curveball. But when we're hypercritical of ourselves, we start to blame any hiccup on ourselves. Even when we do well at something, we aren't capable of acknowledging our own success because we're actively trying to seek something to criticize about ourselves. This is the real threat to our self-worth because if we can't celebrate our success, then we won't feel worthy.

Instead of celebrating, we criticize our efforts even when they're successful! This criticism comes in the form of negative self-talk. Negative self-talk is a dialog you have with yourself that is hypercritical. Negative self-talk can prevent you from trying things. For instance, your inner critic may say you won't succeed at something you want to do, such as applying for a job. The result is that you won't apply for the job, because your inner voice tells you there's no point. Negative self-talk can also make you question your success. Let's say you've completed a project at work. You may have done a good job, but your inner critic will tell you that you've failed. This can lead to perfectionism to the extent that no matter what you do, it won't feel like it's good enough. The result may be that you will end up procrastinating due to fear of failure. You may go the other way, and work too hard on a project, going over time, letting other tasks slip in your desperation to do better.

Negative self-talk can take over all aspects of our lives. Our relationship can suffer if our inner critic tells us we aren't good enough for love. We may begin to suspect our loved ones of cheating on us because we won't feel like we're enough for them. Being self-critical may make you appear insecure and even needy if you turn to your partner for the approval you can't get from yourself. Negative self-talk can turn many of your other thoughts into negativity, leading to a fatalistic mindset. You may begin to see the world through a negative lens, which can lead to depressive thoughts and a downward spiral. In turn, this could lead to significant mental health problems such as clinical depression and anxiety.

COMPARING OURSELVES TO OTHERS AND SOCIAL MEDIA

We might think it's healthy to try to live up to the high standards set by other people we admire. After all, if we have a low opinion of ourselves, it may seem logical to emulate someone we consider to be more successful than we are. It's normal to look up to people. Some friends, relatives or acquaintances might appear to be doing better than we are. We may think that if we can only emulate them, we might also be successful. The trouble is when we compare ourselves to others, we aren't comparing ourselves to something that's real. Most people only show you the best of themselves. Most people are more likely to talk about their successes than their failures. A fellow parent is probably quite happy to tell you how their son made it onto the little league team. They're less likely to tell you that the same child is failing math at school because they have trouble concentrating in class. Or a friend who tells you they are getting a pay rise may not tell you they've failed to reach their monthly sales quota. What you know of many people is only half the story. If you compare yourself unfavorably to the friend who got a pay rise you're doing yourself a disservice. So, unless you know everything that is going on in someone's life, it's best not to compare yourself to them because, in all likelihood, their life isn't as perfect as it seems.

Comparing yourself to people on social media is even less reliable than comparing yourself to people from your real life. Celebrities, social influencers and even your friends and family only share the best parts of their lives on social media. The mom who posts pictures of herself surrounded by happy, smiling children might have been in tears just moments before the photo was taken because her children were misbehaving. Posts on social media are only a tiny snapshot of the whole picture.

CHAPTER SUMMARY

- By overachieving, seeking perfection, being super busy and setting high standards can backfire as ways to increase self-worth. For example, trying to be too perfect can mean you are never happy even when you succeed.
- Trying to compete with others and those we follow on social media can make us feel worse, lowering our sense of self-worth even further.

In the next chapter, you will learn….

- How being too busy leads to stress
- How being too busy affects the workplace
- How being too busy kills creativity
- How being too busy stops you from improving
- How being busy isn't the answer to improving your sense of self-worth

CHAPTER FOUR

THE HARMFUL EFFECTS OF BUSYNESS

Many people seem to enjoy being busy. For some, it's in their nature to be on the go all the time. For others, it's just the by-product of a demanding career or lifestyle. But busyness can be dangerous. Being busy can paper over the cracks. For those struggling with a low sense of self-worth, whether temporarily or permanently, it can be a symptom of a larger problem. Making themselves as busy as possible is one way for people to try to feel better about themselves. By continuously keeping themselves occupied, filling every minute of the day with seemingly worthwhile and productive acts, people are very often doing the opposite of increasing their sense of self-worth.

BUSYNESS AND STRESS

Our reaction to stress is instinctual. When we're stressed, our body thinks we're in danger and it reacts with a fight or flight response. We respond to stress in exactly the same way as we would to a real, physical threat such as coming face to face with a dangerous animal like a lion. When we're stressed our adrenaline spikes—in dangerous situations this is so we are able to move away from the threat quickly.

Endorphins are also released, our muscles tighten, our heart rate goes up and our senses become hypersensitive. This response is incredibly useful when we're in danger. You need to be able to move quickly when you're being chased down by a lion. It's less useful for situations we can't or don't need to escape from. In everyday, stressful situations, this stress response isn't so useful. Because we haven't released our stress, stress hormones build up. As stress hormones continue to rise we can end up experiencing chronic stress.

Chronic stress can have a negative impact on the body. Stress hormones cause your blood vessels to tighten in order to send oxygen to your muscles. This can raise your blood pressure, which will put your heart under pressure over time and increases the risk of a heart attack. Continuous stress weakens your immune system, which can lead to infections and illness. Chronic stress can also lead to diabetes because the fight or flight response causes the release of glucose into your blood for fuel. If too much glucose is released through stress your blood sugar levels can skyrocket.

THE EFFECTS OF BEING BUSY ON THE WORKPLACE

People with low self-worth may take on more work than their colleagues as a way to garner favor or praise from bosses or colleagues. This busyness at work can backfire in a number of ways. Being in competition with workmates can cause hostility, especially if your busyness makes them look bad by comparison. In their desperation to feel needed, wanted or in demand, people who try to take on too much may end up doing a worse job. Being too busy at work can cause exhaustion. Being exhausted means you're more likely to make mistakes in the workplace. Not only is this bad for productivity, but it can also be dangerous. According to the CDC,[10] when workers are on the job for more than forty hours, injuries increased by 23%. When people try to squeeze in more work during a normal shift this can be just as detrimental. Trying to do too much in a short time means we can't commit one hundred percent to any one task. Taking on too many jobs for the time you have available can result in missing deadlines or not delivering the quality or quantity of work as promised, as well as disappointing and losing customers. Setting your goals too high at work will lead to disappointment for you and will only serve to confirm your own low sense of self-worth. This may cause you to try to take on even more work than before until you become so busy and stressed that you reach a breaking point. Burnout and even clinical depression or anxiety disorders might result if you put yourself under this sort of strain for too long.

BEING TOO BUSY KILLS CREATIVITY

If you're busy, your mind tends to be busy, occupied with having to juggle doing too many things at once. This leaves little room for thinking about anything else. One study[11] tested subjects on a word association test. Those who were given less to do were more creative in their answers, whereas those who had additional tasks were less creative in their answers. What this means is that if an individual

---

[10] "Overtime and Extended Work Shifts - CDC." https://www.cdc.gov/niosh/docs/2004-143/pdfs/2004-143.pdf. Accessed 24 Jun. 2021.
[11] "Why Being Constantly Busy Is Killing Your Creativity | Inc.com." 1 Jul. 2016, https://www.inc.com/jessica-stillman/being-constantly-busy-is-killing-your-creativity-study-says.html. Accessed 24 Jun. 2021.

doesn't have enough downtime, they're less creative. Having a busy mind, full of thoughts about having lots to do, leaves less brainpower to come up with new ideas. This means that if you're too busy, you're unlikely to be able to produce anything unique or interesting in your workplace. This makes it less likely for you to stand out and move up within your workplace. If the point of being busy is to succeed, it may pay to take a little more time out to relax! Our brains, it turns out, need time out in order to function optimally. Some brain functions need downtime to function properly. For instance, downtime is essential for the brain's memory, attention, and motivation.[12] It may be that downtime may be crucial to normal brain function in a similar way that sleep is. At the very least, lack of downtime from being too busy may leave your thoughts foggy and confused. It may affect your decision-making and the ability to regulate your emotions.

BUSYNESS BLOCKS YOUR IMPROVEMENT

Your brain is so crammed full of your "to do" list that you can barely think of anything else. Not giving your brain a moment to contemplate anything means you have less opportunity to prioritize what's important in your life, to look at alternative paths or ways of doing things. You become very blinkered, just going about your tasks mindlessly. This means you don't give yourself the chance to better yourself or your situation. In a way, you become stuck in a cycle of busyness that gets you nowhere. If you don't have time to look at the

---

[12] "Why Chronic Busyness Is Bad for Your Brain | Inc.com." 15 Apr. 2014, https://www.inc.com/jessica-stillman/why-chronic-busyness-is-bad-for-the-brain.html. Accessed 24 Jun. 2021.

possibilities all around you it means missing out on opportunities. For instance, you might not have a moment to consider whether you want to do something else with your life. A change in career or your environment won't occur to you even if your life may be vastly improved because you're just too busy. Make time to reassess your life, your goals and you at least have the chance to make better decisions about your future. Take the time to assess your progress and check with yourself from time to time in order to see where you're headed and you can find out what will make you happy. Don't bury yourself in work. Let yourself just be.

WHY WE LOVE BEING BUSY

Being busy can feel like a form of altruism. Being busy is a way of helping others. Running around after your children, doing extra hours for your boss, taking work calls and emails from home, it all makes you seem like you're doing a lot for other people. But you're also doing it for yourself. It's not just that you want to improve your success levels, be more productive, and get work done when you're super busy. There's something else driving you to such lengths. You want to prove to the world that you're worth it. You also want to prove to yourself that you're worthy.

In fact, many people act busy to cover up for their feelings of inadequacy. Their busyness is a survival technique against the pain and shame they feel inside because of their low self-worth. They believe that if they are busy for long periods, they can prove to others (and to themselves) that they have worth. This is a very easy cognitive dissonance to fall into in a capitalistic world that likes to assign a monetary value to everything. Hence, busyness, for many people with low self-esteem, is a way to assign a monetary value to their efforts. Their thought process goes: "If I am able to make a lot of money and continue to move up in my career, then I will finally have value in this world."

Indeed it is very easy to fall into this trap, even for people with healthy self-esteem. Busyness and our overwork culture work hand in hand to remind us daily that we can tie our identity in how much work we do. If we do plenty of work, we are good enough. If we stop to rest or enjoy a hobby that brings us no monetary value, we are not good enough. Busyness is also easy. It can be an easy, if rather unbalanced, option to work your way up the ladder in many sectors if you neglect your friends, family, and your health and sacrifice it all to make money for your company and your industry. At the end of your journey, you can then count the fruits of your labor in the form of monetary value. But taking time to spend with a loved one has no tangible value. It is also more difficult to learn how to connect with others in a healthy way, to respect their boundaries while still making sure you love them and are there for them. Taking time off for yourself and your loved ones requires fluidity, self-awareness, and self-love.

You will also find that being busy stops you from contemplating why you have such a low sense of self-worth in the first place. Earlier in this book, we talked about the causes of low self-worth. Many of those causes are deeply rooted in childhood or later traumatic experiences. They may stem from experiences you might not want to think about. You may not be able to face the reality of why you don't think you're worthy. Being busy won't help you escape whatever it is that has robbed you of your feeling of self-worth. Being busy won't solve the underlying problem. Low self-worth won't be solved by "doing." You won't gain self-worth by running around trying to please other people. You will only build your self-worth by working on improving the way you feel about yourself. This may sound scary. But we're convinced you will feel so much better once you learn the truth. Because the truth is you are worth it. You are worthy. You just have to learn to believe it. You don't have to go on this journey alone. We're here to help you every step of the way.

CHAPTER SUMMARY

- Being overly busy causes stress, which can eventually be damaging to our bodies.
- Being too busy can cause problems in the workplace. For example, taking on too many tasks at one time makes it difficult to do a good job.
- Being too busy kills creativity. Having too much to do can stop the thought processes that lead to creativity.
- Busyness blocks improvement by giving us little time to look for opportunities.
- Being busy seems like doing good, but the only way to improve your self-worth is to work on how you feel about yourself.

In the next chapter, you will learn….

- about the physical impact of having a low sense of self-worth
- about the emotional and psychological ramifications of feeling unworthy

CHAPTER FIVE

THE DAMAGING IMPACT OF LOW SELF-WORTH

Low self-worth isn't just a feeling. It affects you all of the time. It affects how you act and the decisions you make. It also affects you on a deeper level, emotionally and psychologically, which can lead to physical issues as well.

THE PHYSICAL IMPACT OF LOW SELF-WORTH

Anxiety is a common result of having a low sense of self-worth. Low self-worth makes an individual feel hopeless. If you aren't very good at things, or if you don't feel like you can influence people, it can feel like you don't have much control over your life. A low opinion of yourself means you don't think people approve of you. This means you may be a people pleaser who tries to take on too many tasks to make people like you. You also continually worry about whether or not your efforts are good enough. Therefore, you continue to outdo your own best efforts, fearing that you will be rejected. The strain of trying to please may lead to anxiety; clinical anxiety can be crippling. Living in a state of continual anxiety will put your body under strain. This continual physical stress may lead to panic attacks. Panic attacks can be scary. They can hit at any time and are characterized by a racing heart, sweating, shaking, palpitations, numbness, shortness of breath and an unsettling feeling of impending doom. It may feel like you're having a heart attack and many people can end up in the hospital due to a panic attack. This may only serve to increase the sense of being unworthy. You may feel bad for wasting people's time, and you may be embarrassed for overreacting. If you suffer panic attacks, it's important to know that when one happens it's not your fault. It's a normal reaction to extreme stress. Once you have the tools to disrupt your panic attack, you can take back control.

Another common result of having a low sense of self-worth is insomnia. Being filled with feelings of self-loathing and fear of failure can make it difficult to sleep. People with low self-worth may relive their failures, trying to figure out where they went wrong. Sometimes these thoughts can keep you awake at night. This only serves to make you exhausted during the day, making you prone to making mistakes, which further degrades your sense of self-worth and fills your nights with thoughts of failure. Having low self-worth can make you feel like no one likes you. This can make you feel shy, withdrawn, or nervous around people. This anxiety can lead you to feel embarrassed or ashamed about your lack of social skills. Thinking about how you may have embarrassed yourself in a social situation may also keep you awake at night.

PHYSICAL PAIN

People who feel good about themselves often carry themselves with pride. Their shoulders are back, their head is up and they stride forward with confidence. People with low self-worth, in contrast, can tend to slump or hunch their shoulders and look downward. This bad posture can have a marked effect on your body. Your head is heavy and when it drops forward, this can put a lot of strain on your neck. Slumped shoulders can lead to further neck and shoulder pain. Slumped shoulders can lead to weakness that can lead to pain and RSI (Repetitive Strain Injury) in the arms. Being out of balance at the top of your body leads to upper back pain. When posture issues go on it can lead to problems lower down. If lower back pain results this can be more serious. Sciatica may develop and it can become painful to do everyday tasks. Sometimes this pain can become bad enough through continued strain and weakness that it leads to having to take time off work. This can lead to further feelings of anxiety and only decreases the sense of self-worth. Pain can lead to low mood, leading to mood disorders like depression and too much time spent recuperating might lead to decreased fitness, weight gain, and even diabetes. It may seem dramatic to say that a bad posture and slouching can be serious, but as you can see, posture is important. In fact, the role of posture in preventing injury has been well established by multiple studies.[13] So, put your shoulders back, stand tall and walk proudly!

THE EMOTIONAL AND PSYCHOLOGICAL IMPACT OF HAVING LOW SELF-WORTH

People with low self-worth experience a variety of emotional issues as a result. There's a strong correlation between having low self-worth

---

[13] "The Role of Exercise and Posture in Preventing ... - SAGE Journals." http://journals.sagepub.com/doi/pdf/10.1177/216507999003800703. Accessed 26 Jun. 2021.

and being diagnosed with depression. People with low self-worth tend to feel like they aren't likable or good at anything. They tend to feel like they won't amount to much and as such, they feel like their future is bleak. Having a pessimistic view of the future can lead to a feeling of hopelessness. All of these emotions can lead to feelings of depression. It's not nice to feel like you aren't a good person. If a person's sense of self-worth becomes low enough, they may start to feel like they're worthless. This mixture of feeling worthless, useless, not good enough, and helpless can lead to a low mood. As the feeling of being worthless grows, a person may start to feel like there's no point in trying anymore. What's the point in going to school, or work, or even getting out of bed if nothing you do will make any difference? Depression can result if someone with a low sense of self-worth ends up feeling like there's no point in trying anymore.

Not everyone who has a low sense of self-worth will end up having depression. Some may turn to illicit substances to lift their mood and try to make themselves feel better. In a way, people who are starting to feel down about themselves may self-medicate in order to make themselves feel better. Drug-taking and alcohol abuse are common ways for people who don't have a high opinion of themselves to cope with feeling worthless. Some people who have a low sense of self-worth may have trouble socializing. They may use drugs and alcohol in order to make it easier to talk to people. Risk-taking can result as individuals try to make up for their perceived worthlessness. In order to feel brave, to gain attention, or to simply feel something other than useless, some people with a low sense of self-worth may exhibit risky behavior. For instance, they may drink and drive. Feeling worthless can make people more easily led. In order to try to please people, they may end up doing things they normally wouldn't do (for instance, stealing, drug-taking, or sexual promiscuity). If this behavior goes against their morals or beliefs it may lead to an increased sense of being worthless.

Having a low sense of self-worth can trigger generalized anxiety disorder. Feeling worthless leads to feeling helpless which can result in a sense of impending doom. This can make a person feel like bad things are going to happen to them. Not feeling good about your own personality and likability means not trusting other people's opinions of you. You may begin to worry about what other people think of you and fear failing them. This can make you anxious and the need to please can make you try too hard, go the extra mile and wear yourself out trying to do better. Anxiety will begin to take over as the negative self-talk tells you everything you do is not good enough. The harder you try, the less happy you are with your own success. This leads to further anxiety, stress, lack of sleep, and in the end full generalized anxiety may develop. According to the Diagnostic and Statistical Manual of Mental Disorders (DSM5) Generalized Anxiety Disorder (GAD), is diagnosed when there is excessive worry about certain topics, events, or activities for at least six months.

A particular type of anxiety disorder that relates to socializing can also happen to people who have a low sense of self-worth. Feeling bad about who you are can make you feel shy around people. If you don't like yourself, why would anyone else? If you aren't worthy, how can anything you say be worth listening to? This kind of negative self-talk can make social situations crippling. If your self-worth makes you so

41

anxious about talking to people that you can no longer participate in conversations, or if conversations fill you with such dread or if you're overwhelmed by panic when you are in a social situation you may well be experiencing social phobia or social anxiety. Social phobia or social anxiety goes beyond being just a bit shy. People with social phobia can get to the point where they can't even talk when they're around people. They may have a panic attack in social situations. Social phobia, like any phobia, means there are strong physical symptoms of fear such as a racing heart, excessive sweating, a blank mind, sore stomach, muscle pain or ache and trouble breathing. These symptoms only make social situations even worse. It's hard to talk to people if your mind goes blank or if you can't catch your breath! Of course, if you experience this kind of panic in a social situation it will only make your social phobia even worse.

Many other psychological disorders might have their origins in a low sense of self-worth. Sometimes when people don't have a good sense of self-worth they could find themselves imagining what it would be like to be someone who is worthy. If someone's sense of self-worth is so low, this might cause them deep, psychological pain. When individuals have troubling emotions, thoughts and mental anguish, their subconscious finds ways to help them. One way might be to create a personality that is worthy. Dissociative Identity Disorder (formerly known as multiple personality disorder) occurs when there are two or more split personalities within one person. DID is said to be caused by childhood trauma, abuse, or overwhelming experiences. These experiences are so traumatic that they are said to prevent a unified sense of self. In the case of people who have a low sense of self-worth, it may be that the split personality occurs to make up for a sense of worthlessness. The split personality might be funnier, more outgoing, more courageous, or even more intelligent and in control, which would make this personality more worthy.

Bipolar Disorder is characterized by periods of depressive symptoms followed by periods of mania and hypomania. When in a depressive phase, individuals can feel so low in emotion and mood that they can barely manage to get out of bed, dress, or eat. During the manic stage, the opposite is true and individuals can end up hyperactive and on the go for days at a time, going without sleep and being on the go nonstop. The mood during mania is characterized by increased self-confidence, extreme risk-taking, bad judgment, grandiose ideas and thoughts, racing thoughts and speech, euphoria, an upbeat mood and decreased need for sleep. It's possible that having a low sense of self-worth could contribute to having bipolar disorder. Feeling depressed and low is often experienced by people who have a low sense of self-worth. The manic phase of bipolar disorder may well be the mind's way of snapping the mind out of this low state. The manic phase will allow people who have a low sense of self-worth to feel good about themselves. Grandiose thoughts, extreme self-confidence and euphoria will allow them to feel good about themselves. The mania of the "up phase" of bipolar disorder simply won't allow people to feel worthless.

Feelings of worthlessness can lead people to judge their physical appearance harshly especially in comparison to the perfect images they see of people on social media. This can lead to eating disorders like bulimia and anorexia. As people with a low sense of self-worth are

43

more sensitive to feelings of inadequacy, this makes them more vulnerable to eating disorders as they associate their physical image with their lack of worthiness. Feeling overweight can give people with a low sense of self-worth an overwhelming sense of anxiety and shame. In order to feel better about themselves they may start to obsess over their weight and become fixated on the idea of losing weight. For someone with a low sense of self-worth, being able to control their weight may be one of the few ways they can take control of their sense of self-worth. As they start to feel better about themselves after losing weight, they may end up trying to increase this short-term boost of confidence by continuing to diet. A high proportion of people who suffer from eating disorders are likely to suffer from a low sense of self-worth as well.

Not only does having a low sense of self-worth contribute to the development of mental disorders, but mental disorders may also lead to a low sense of self-worth. For instance, having ADHD may lead someone to have a low opinion of their own worth. ADHD causes children and adults to have difficulty in school and society at large. Attention and hyperactivity problems can lead to difficulty concentrating, staying on task and sitting still or listening. This makes doing well in school and in the workplace challenging. Feeling like a failure in school and in the workplace can contribute to a feeling of being worthless, especially when teachers and peers may respond negatively to the behavioral symptoms of ADHD.

CHAPTER SUMMARY

- A low sense of self-worth can lead to physical problems. For example, anxiety can lead to heart palpitations. Back and other pain can arise from the bad posture that comes from feeling unworthy.

- Many serious emotional and psychological problems can arise out of feeling unworthy. For instance, clinical depression can occur due to feeling bad about yourself.

In the next chapter, you will learn....

- how to gain perspective by changing the way you treat yourself
- how understanding the truth about being perfect will help your perspective
- how positive thinking will help you get perspective
- how logic and distance will help you change your perspective
- how learning to see things from other people's perspectives will help you

CHAPTER SIX

GAINING PERSPECTIVE

Gaining perspective means seeing the big picture. Our perspective is colored by our experiences. When we have bad experiences, these can skew our thoughts towards negativity. If our perspective makes us listen to negative self-talk this negative self-talk can take over. We can start to view every event negatively. When good things happen we can fob them off, or give them less weight than negative events. For example, if we managed to reach a sales target, instead of feeling good about our sales skills we might tell ourselves that the customers would have bought the product or service anyway and that it had nothing to do with us. If we have done well, our negative self-talk may tell us that it was just a fluke. If something bad happened that was out of our control, we might put the blame on ourselves. For instance, someone on the outside looking in at our life and our achievements would see these examples more objectively. They would realize that the failure that occurred was the result of an occurrence that was outside of our control. They would also see that meeting sales targets requires people skills, time, effort and knowledge to achieve. They would tell you not to feel bad about something you can't control and they would tell you that you should feel good about positive outcomes due to your efforts.

GAIN PERSPECTIVE BY TREATING YOURSELF AS YOU WOULD A FRIEND

If your friend told you they were useless, would you agree with them? No, you wouldn't. You would probably tell them they've had some bad luck or that they have just run into a few bumps that are not their fault. So, why not cut yourself the same slack. The reason is that your low sense of self-worth has told you you don't deserve to be treated well—even by yourself. But guess what? You do deserve to be treated with kindness—especially by you. In order to gain perspective on your life you need to learn to view it the way you would view a friend's life. It's sometimes easier for us to see the truth behind someone else's problems or issues. This is because we see their life from the outside. Our views aren't clouded by their history; all we have is the facts. Now, in order to have the same perspective on your own life you need to face your issues with the same sense of logic. You need to learn to silence the negative voice in your head that immediately jumps to the wrong conclusion. It will be difficult. You've probably been listening to your negative self-talk for a long time. But you can do it. In the next chapter, we'll show you how.

GAIN PERSPECTIVE BY UNDERSTANDING NO ONE IS AS PERFECT AS THEY SEEM

It may seem like everyone else is perfect. Maybe other people around you get their work done more quickly. Maybe some of them stay at work late in order to get things done. Maybe a colleague who started with a company at the same time as you managed to climb the ranks at the workplace when you're still exactly where you started. It would be natural to wonder what is wrong with you and to conclude you simply are not as good at your job as everyone else. But this is most likely not to be the case. You are probably concentrating too much on your own failures instead of considering the struggles of other people. The colleague who stays late each day to get their work done isn't necessarily more diligent than you are, in fact, they may not be very efficient and let their work pile on top of them, or perhaps they are more productive towards the end of the day when it is quieter in the office. They may have less going on in their lives than you do. Perhaps they live alone and don't have family commitments. They may think of their job as the most important thing in their life, whereas you may have other hobbies or commitments that keep you from putting in too many hours on the job. In fact, having a more balanced work and personal life is far healthier for you, both physically and mentally. We all have different ways of working and you should manage your role in the way which feels most comfortable for you; as long as you produce the work expected of you then you are doing a great job!

GAIN PERSPECTIVE BY THINKING POSITIVELY

If you have a low sense of self-worth you may have formed a pattern of thinking negatively about yourself so that no matter what you do you end up coming up with a negative perception of your actions. In order to unlearn this try to immediately debunk your own negative self-talk by turning your thoughts positive. For instance, an individual who thinks they are not good at making friends will think that their lack of social life is caused by their unlikeable personality. Putting a positive

49

spin on this thought will change their perspective. A more positive interpretation of having no social life would be to consider less judgmental reasons. For instance, when a person is shy they may stay away from places where they will need to socialize, which means there is less chance for them to make friends. It is not their personality that prevents friendship from occurring; it's their avoidance behavior.

APPLY LOGIC TO THE SITUATION

Stepping back and looking at situations logically can help you gain perspective by stripping away the emotions and negative self-interpretation. If there's a situation in your life that you think you may be using negative self-talk to interpret, try to look at it logically.

For instance, take the problem of having a limited social life. Firstly, apply your usual thinking to the problem. Now try to debunk that thinking with logic. Finally, and this is the good part, try to use logic to find a solution.

Situation: Lack of social life.

Cause: Not being very good at socializing.

Logical explanation: Staying away from social situations means there's little or no opportunity to make friends.

Logical solution: Try to socialize more. Start with small gatherings. Join a club, start a new hobby or join a group in order to meet new people in a way that is fun with little pressure.

The problem with listening to negative self-talk for situations is that it allows for little positive change. In this case, simply concluding that not being good at socializing offered no solution. Whereas using logic leads to a positive solution.

CREATE SOME DISTANCE TO GAIN PERSPECTIVE

If you are emotionally invested in something, it's hard to judge it objectively. Try not to place too much emotional value on your role in everyday situations. As a parent, for instance, you might take it personally if your child misbehaves, isn't happy, doesn't settle, or doesn't listen to you. Just like us, children have bad days. When your child has a tantrum or cries or screams in public, this doesn't mean you're a bad parent. Other factors can come into play when determining your child's behavior, such as temperament and age (it's called the terrible twos for a reason). If you're struggling as a parent it doesn't mean you have failed or aren't good at it. A number of factors can contribute to whether or not you struggle as a parent. For a start, most parents find things tough at some point; many refer to it as the hardest job in the world—rewarding, yes, but hard! If you feel like you aren't coping, don't blame yourself. You may have less support than others. Your child may struggle for physical reasons, such as colic. In this case, try to gain some perspective by gaining distance from the situation. Think of your child's behavior as separate from you. You are not failing, or a bad parent, because of your child's behavior.

SEEK OUT OTHER PERSPECTIVES

Sometimes we're too invested in a situation to view things objectively. It can be hard to take a step back from a situation and see it logically. In this case, it can be helpful to seek an outside perspective. Is there someone you can trust to talk to about a situation? Is there a close friend, family member, spiritual adviser, doctor or therapist that you can be open and honest with who won't judge you? Your chosen confidant should be trusted to be fair, honest and non-judgmental. Most of all they should be trusted to keep what they tell you to themselves. Sometimes it may be easier to talk to a professional so that they can view your situation objectively. Once you give this person the facts, they should be able to tell you the objective truth. Sometimes you may not know if you are being hard on yourself. You may know you're giving in to negative self-talk but you may need someone else's help in finding a different perspective on the situation. It might be hard to reach out to another person and talk about the things you don't feel good about. You may fear that they will simply agree with your negative self-talk. This is unlikely to be the case. Your negative self-talk is stopping you from feeling good about yourself. Someone else is likely to see the good in you that you haven't been able to see. Let them help you. You may be surprised to learn the truth about yourself: that you are worthy!

CHAPTER SUMMARY:

Revisit the key points of the chapter in bullet point format. (Example below)

- Treating yourself as you would treat a friend will allow you to go easier on yourself and see things more kindly and clearly.
- Learning that no one is perfect will put your own life into perspective; imperfection is normal.
- Positive thoughts will shift your perspective from negative to being positive and more open.
- Logic lets you analyze situations, giving you a truer perspective.
- Creating distance helps you see things more clearly and without emotion.
- Seeking out other perspectives, from friends, for example, will help you see the truth about yourself and your life.

In the next chapter, you will learn....

- How to evaluate situations objectively
- How to turn negative self-talk into positive self-talk in order to evaluate situations more fairly
- How to assess whether this new perspective is correct and validate it

CHAPTER SEVEN

EVALUATE AND VALIDATE SITUATIONS OBJECTIVELY

With your newfound ability to gain perspective on things, you should be able to evaluate and validate situations more objectively. In the past, you may have instantly listened to the negative self-talk in order to evaluate situations. Now though, you know to take your time before jumping to conclusions. Stopping yourself from instantly listening to negative self-talk will allow you to practice what you've learned about gaining perspective on situations before you act. Even though you know the theory behind thinking about things more objectively, old habits die hard. You might have a lifetime of listening to your negative self-talk. Negative self-talk happens on the subconscious level. When this happens our negative self-talk can elicit an emotional response. It's more difficult to think logically when we're emotional. So, if you find yourself in a situation where you are feeling emotional, try to take a moment to pause before acting or jumping to conclusions. Remember to take yourself through the steps that will help you gain perspective and see things clearly.

The ability to evaluate situations objectively takes practice and time. In the beginning, it may help you to keep a diary to write about how you've managed to think objectively. In your diary, you could write about the negative self-talk that occurred. Hopefully, you were successful in dismissing the negative self-talk. If so, well done! Write this down in your diary. Don't feel bad if negative self-talk got the better of you on this occasion. It can be hard to recognize when negative self-talk is derailing you. That's what this exercise is for, to teach you when to deny the thoughts that aren't worth listening to.

> Situation: My boss didn't give me a raise at work, but they gave a raise to my colleague.

> Negative self-talk: I'm not good at my job. My boss doesn't like me. I'm a failure. I may as well stop trying so hard, I'll never get anywhere in life.

> Positive Self-talk: There will be a good explanation for why my colleague got a raise when I didn't.

> Assess the situation objectively: Can you think of a good explanation for why your colleague got the raise?

My colleague went to school with my boss and they are good friends outside of work. This means they probably gave my colleague a raise because they're friends.

Validate your objective assessment: Being friends means my boss has a reason to reward my colleague. As we aren't friends, they have less reason to give me a raise. My boss's relationship with my colleague has given them a positive bias toward my colleague.

In this example, you can see that with further thought and investigation it was easy to debunk the negative self-talk. Sometimes our negative self-talk can make us jump to conclusions that seem to support a low sense of self-worth. This then can make our sense of self-worth even lower. It's a cycle that's hard to break out of, but you're well on your way to learning how.

See if you can try to use what you've learned in the previous chapter about gaining a perspective to help you assess situations more objectively and then use the skills you've learned to validate a more positive conclusion.

Remember the methods we learned about in the previous chapter to gain a better perspective of our lives and the situations we face:

- Treat yourself like a friend
- Remember no one is perfect
- Turn negative thoughts into positive ones
- Use logic to analyze situations
- Create distance to gain perspective
- Seek out other perspectives

Try to use the above ideas to help you assess situations more objectively. You can write about this in your diary. Some solutions will be more useful in different situations. For instance, it may be useful to create distance in an emotional situation by taking time out (e.g., go for a walk or do some deep breathing) so that you can react with a clearer head.

Here is an example of how you might use these different methods to help you assess situations more objectively.

Monday:

I didn't manage to make my sales target this week.

NEGATIVE SELF-TALK

I'm obviously no good at this job.

Assess this using one of the solutions you've learned about:

Treat yourself like a friend. If your friend came to you and said they aren't any good at the job of salesperson because they didn't make their weekly target, what would you say?

"There is always next week. It's bad luck you probably came across some hard-to-please customers."

Now, tell yourself the same thing.

By treating yourself with the same kindness as you would a friend, you have just managed to prove to yourself that you aren't bad at your job.

Tuesday:

I didn't make my goal weight this week. In fact, I put on weight.

Negative self-talk: I will never lose weight. I will always be overweight. I may as well not try to eat well at all.

ASSESS THIS USING ONE OF THE SOLUTIONS YOU'VE LEARNED ABOUT

Remember no one is perfect.

If you are part of a group that meets for weigh-ins, are you the only one who has not met their weight loss goal? There are probably others who have also had a small step back in their weight loss journey. If you are on a weight loss journey by yourself, rest assured it's normal to slip up every now and then. Life can sometimes get in the way and we lose focus on our goals. No one is perfect all of the time. It's best to look at your progress over a longer period and remember that all the small positive changes to eating healthily and taking more exercise will improve your overall health and ultimately lead to a more healthy weight. Also, remember that everyone's body is different and things like water retention can artificially inflate your weight. Likewise, muscle weighs more than fat, so if you have been exercising and see a weight increase it might be that you have swapped fat for muscle, which is heavier but healthier! Remember to gain perspective and try to evaluate objectively, rather than emotionally.

Validation: This was a hard week at work, which has made me tired and I ended up eating more than I needed to, as well as having too many sugary snacks. Understanding that no one is perfect will help you understand that it's okay to slip up sometimes. It doesn't make you less worthy than others because they too will fail every now and then.

You are upset that your neighbor is having a barbeque that they invited everyone to except for you.

Negative self-talk: You thought your neighbors liked you and enjoyed your company. Obviously, you were wrong. They don't like you. You are unpopular. No one will ever like you. From now on you will ignore your neighbors and keep to yourself.

ASSESS THE SITUATION

Assess the situation by creating distance to gain perspective. Go and listen to some music or go for a walk to clear your head. Once removed from the situation that is upsetting you try to think about it logically. Is there any reason why your neighbors didn't invite you to the barbeque? Perhaps you could hold your judgment before you decide they don't like you. Wait until you see them again to find out if there's a good explanation.

VALIDATION

After waiting it turns out one of your neighbors thought you were going on holiday during the barbeque. They were mistaken and felt bad about not inviting you, so they threw a barbeque just for you.

What you will have learned from this example is that had you listened to your negative self-talk, you would have made the wrong decision in turning your back on your neighbors. By taking a step back, cooling off you were able to find out the truth.

Here you can see how negative self-talk can make you see things that aren't true and jump to the wrong conclusion.

CHAPTER SUMMARY

Revisit the key points of the chapter in bullet point format. (Example below)

- If you find yourself giving in to negative self-talk, acknowledge it.
- Reassess the situation with a more positive perspective. In this way, you can find alternative explanations for situations that you viewed negatively.
- Validate your more positive and realistic explanation by using evidence and logic.

In the next chapter, you will learn....

- How working harder doesn't always result in greater success
- How working smarter will get you more success than working harder
- Ways to work smarter

CHAPTER EIGHT

WORK SMARTER NOT HARDER

We're taught that if we work hard we will reap the rewards. The longer we work, the more we'll get paid, the more work will be done and the more highly we will be regarded. It makes sense. So that's what we often do. Working hard can mean working extra shifts, long hours, taking work home with you, missing lunch breaks and doing extra unpaid work in order to get ahead. The result of this "hard work" is often burnout, stress, anxiety, lack of sleep, lack of focus. Mistakes happen when people work for too many hours or try to do too much at once. So, is it worth it? Does working hard get us more than working a moderate amount? The answer, in most cases, is no. Often people who work harder at their job end up getting the same amount of pay even though they've done more work. Going the extra mile at work doesn't always pay off in terms of rewards. In fact, doing more sometimes does little more than set the bar higher for yourself. If you work extra hard one week your employer may think you should work just as hard the next week for the same reward! So all you've done in working harder is make life more difficult for yourself.

So if working harder isn't the best way, how else will you get ahead in life? The answer is that instead of working harder you need to work smarter. Working smarter means that you must employ tactics that make the best use of your time and get the job done as efficiently as possible. Often this may mean thinking outside of the box and coming up with strategies that help you get things done faster, better and with less effort.

A classic example of working smarter not harder is Henry Ford's production line. Henry Ford revolutionized the assembly line by adding a conveyor belt to it in 1913.[14] This meant workers didn't have to leave their seats and move about in order to do their work. The assembly line sped up the production of the automobile so much that it became so much easier and cheaper to make. The famous model T that came out of this innovation changed the world of vehicular travel forever, turning cars from luxury items to something nearly everyone could own. Just like the assembly line, we too can make our working and everyday lives easier by working smarter.

WAYS TO WORK SMARTER

1. Automate your tasks. We make a lot of decisions throughout the day, and each one of these decisions takes time and energy. By automating a lot of our daily routines, we can cut out the effort, time and energy they take. Set a certain day to do tasks a certain way. When you do your laundry, for

---

[14] "Ford's assembly line starts rolling — History.com This Day."
https://www.history.com/this-day-in-history/fords-assembly-line-starts-rolling.
Accessed 10 Jul. 2021.

WHEN WILL I BE GOOD ENOUGH?

instance, if you make a pile of all your white clothes when it comes time to do the washing all you need do is place the pre-made pile straight into the machine. No sorting is needed. No thinking about what colors you will do. It may sound silly and a little simple, but by making small changes that can free up your time and energy in one area, you are freeing your mind for other areas. Other examples include pre-planning the meals you will cook for the week. You could go one step further and cook bulk meals that can be frozen individually and then freeze them to heat up later.

2. Prioritize important tasks: Your attention is torn in many different directions. There's so much to do and so little time. It can be tempting to put off the hardest things until last. However, this can create a sense of unease. You know the most important thing is the task you should be doing. Procrastination can lead to a habit of not doing the thing that needs to be done the most. One way of making sure you don't leave the most difficult jobs until last is to give yourself a shorter deadline than required. If you have a week to do something that is going to be difficult, it will be natural to tackle easier tasks instead. The result is that you may end up running out of time to do the most important task. You actually may end up rushing it and doing a bad job! So instead give yourself two days to complete the task and stick to this deadline firmly. In all likelihood, this will encourage you to start the task right away. Now that you've got the hardest thing out of the way, the rest of the week will be easier, less stressful

and you won't have that all-important deadline hanging over you. You can relax and get on with the jobs you'd rather be doing. If you put the most important tasks first, focus on only them, then you will be able to put all of your energy where it should be. Beginning one task, then switching to another, leads to less focus, more distraction and possibly having to double up on work later.

3. Do more of what you enjoy. If you find a job that you enjoy, you'll have less stress because your job is more like a hobby than work. If you can find a job that speaks to your interests, the things you do in your spare time may help with your work time. For instance, if you're passionate about science, you are likely to want to learn, read and think about science in your spare time. Your leisure time will feed into your work, making you more knowledgeable, efficient and passionate. Passion is a great motivator. Passion leads to innovation, excitement and joy. Love your work and you will be more productive without even trying.

4. Follow a routine. We're creatures of habit. We feel comfortable with routines. Creating a routine means we don't have to think too much about what we have to do. Planning takes time. If we have a pre-planned routine, we can just get on with our tasks without wasting time. Routines aren't just for work. Our everyday life can be improved by following routines. For instance, if you want to go to the gym in order to get fit, lose weight or get stronger, it pays to follow a routine rather than just going from machine to machine aimlessly.

Your routine will include a plan that is best chosen by a gym instructor or personal trainer. They will analyze your body type, your goals and your fitness level and come up with a routine that will use your time optimally in order for you to reach your goals. A similar outcome can be achieved in many areas of your life. Following a routine is a smarter way to get fit than merely taking a working hard approach. If you just randomly decided to do a lot of running to get fit, you might end up hurting yourself. If you run too far, and too quickly, you may end up pulling a muscle resulting in the inability to do any exercise at all. The same goes for other areas of your life. You will achieve your goal if you plan properly and follow a well-thought-out routine.

5. Be more efficient. Working more efficiently can cut down on time and create less work for you in the end. One way of working more efficiently is to figure which time of day is better suited to which tasks. If you have more energy first thing in the morning take on more difficult tasks that need to be done quickly and that takes energy. Other tasks which require less thinking skills can wait for later in the day when your energy flags. For instance, manual and repetitive tasks that you can do easily. Another way is to figure out if there is a better way of doing your tasks. For instance, are there similar tasks that you can lump together so that you don't need to double up on some of your actions? For example, if you need to print off forms for different jobs, perhaps you can print them all at once instead of going back and forth several times for different jobs.

6. Improve your time management. Time management skills are essential to all areas of life. Start your day by preparing the night before. Deciding what you are going to wear the next day, preparing lunch the day before and packing your bag/briefcase/purse for work can all save you precious time in the morning. If you are late from the start it can set you behind from the start and set off feelings of anxiety. Other ways to improve time management include marking important tasks in a calendar and setting an alarm on your device to remind you of what needs to get done. Making sure you give yourself enough time to do things is an essential time management tool that will save you stress and make your day run smoothly.

CHAPTER SUMMARY

- There are many reasons why working harder results in less success and can even result in failure. For instance, working too hard can lead to burnout, anxiety and stress.

- Working smarter instead of harder can lead to greater success. For example, the assembly line enabled production to speed up significantly.

- There are a number of ways to work smarter. For instance, prioritizing important work and doing what you enjoy to boost enthusiasm.

In the next chapter, you will learn....

- About why comparing yourself to others doesn't work

- About how comparing yourself to others doesn't make you do better

- What to do instead of comparing yourself to others

CHAPTER NINE

STOP COMPARING

Most people aren't as successful as they first appear. In fact, some of the most talented, famous and successful people may feel like failures. Celebrities seem to have it all: fame, money, and the adoration of fans. Yet, many celebrities seem to be at least as unhappy as ordinary people. Famous people can be lonely. They can be socially awkward and quite often have relationship problems. They might often have psychological problems and drug and alcohol addictions. In other words, despite gaining success in their chosen careers, they are just as prone to mishaps and failures in the rest of their lives as the rest of us. This is the key to understanding why comparing yourself to others is futile. People only show the best of themselves on social media.

Celebrities, in particular, have the means to portray their lives in the best light possible. Celebrities can use airbrushing techniques to drastically change the way they look in photographs to the extent that they don't look much like themselves at all. Sometimes airbrushing goes so far as to result in beauty standards that are not only difficult to live up to, they may even be physically impossible to emulate. Many advertising campaigns have been banned because airbrushing creates false images. For instance, a slew of advertisements has been banned due to airbrushing that include the altered images of celebrities like Natalie Portman, Julia Roberts and Cara Delevingne, and Twiggy.[15]

With airbrushing techniques becoming more mainstream, an increasing number of people are now airbrushing their own images. So, next time you see a celebrity or even your old high school rival looking ten years younger than you think you do, bear in mind they may not actually look like that. Even without airbrushing, with good lighting and a perfect shot, we can all look amazing. And that's the point. No one puts the worst of themselves on social media. If you see an advertisement for a celebrity who looks like they have baby smooth skin, resist the urge to feel bad about how your skin might look in comparison. The image you're looking at isn't necessarily a true reflection of real life.

REASONS WHY COMPARING YOURSELF IS BAD

You might think comparing yourself to other people is a good motivator. The problem is that in trying to emulate the achievements of others you may be setting yourself an unrealistic goal. We tend to admire the things in others that we find difficult to achieve. If someone is good at something we find difficult we tend to admire them. It's better for us to try to work with our strengths than to try to become good at something we're not good at.

---

[15] "Cara Delevingne Rimmel mascara ad banned for airbrushing | Cara ...."
https://www.theguardian.com/fashion/2017/apr/19/cara-delevingne-rimmel-mascara-ad-banned-airbrushing. Accessed 11 Jul. 2021.

If you have a low sense of self-worth you probably tend to listen to negative self-talk. Negative self-talk can mean we tend to put great emphasis on our failures. We are less likely to notice when we succeed. When comparing to others we might tend to exaggerate how good they are and we may tend to compare ourselves unfairly, thinking we are worse at something than we really are. When our biases cloud our interpretation of our own success, comparisons are weighted in favor of other people over ourselves. Because we have such a low opinion of ourselves, we are never going to win the comparison game.

Comparing yourself to others can slow down your progress. If you spend your time trying to figure out if someone is better than you or trying to emulate them, you are wasting time that could be spent on your own progress. Learning from others is useful, but if you put too much weight on other people's methods you can end up making things harder for yourself. Instead, learning to do things your own way by finding what's easiest for you will result in greater success. If you become fixated on other people and their ways of doing things, it can lead to feelings of inadequacy. If you feel like you can't compete with someone else, it can damage your motivation.

Comparing yourself to the success of others doesn't show you the journey they undertook to succeed. People usually struggle before they succeed. Sometimes they fail before they succeed. Sometimes they fail a lot! Success doesn't happen overnight. Seeing the end result doesn't tell you what sort of support someone had on their journey to success either. Perhaps a friend, relative or mentor contributed significant help in terms of time, funds, contacts and knowledge. If you had all of the advantages they had, it is possible that you would be just as successful.

Resentment and jealousy can occur when you compare yourself to other people. If you pin your self-esteem and self-worth on the notion of being as good as someone else, when you fail to equal that person, you can come to resent them. This resentment can grow into something unhealthy. Negative feelings toward others, especially if they're not based on negative behaviors by them, can cause us psychological harm. Holding onto dislike or hatred eats away at us, making us feel negative emotions like annoyance and anger. Negative thoughts can have a harmful effect on our mental and physical well-being. Negative thoughts about others that are caused by envy can make us act in ways we normally wouldn't. We might talk about people behind their backs, insult people in public, act rudely and unkindly. These behaviors not only make us feel bad and embarrassed later, but they can also damage our reputation.

WHAT TO DO INSTEAD OF MAKING COMPARISONS

Often there is little we can do about the feeling that someone is better than us. We can try to improve ourselves. But what about when that doesn't work? There will almost always be someone who is better at something than you are. They may have invested more time, effort and energy into their success, or they may simply have had better luck. We can't change that other person, but there's one thing we can change; we can change ourselves. More specifically, we can change our mental view of how we see ourselves compared to other people.

FOCUS ON YOUR STRENGTHS

Negative self-talk and a low sense of self-worth lead to putting too much emphasis on the negative. For our whole lives, we've been taught to seek improvement, to set new goals, to do better. Society pushes us to meet certain criteria. Right from when we first enter grade school to when we graduate and beyond, there are certain standards we must meet. Once we meet them, we barely pause before we're onto the next goal. Finished high school? Move on to college, or an apprenticeship. Once we've succeeded in one area we're taught to move on and look to the next. It's little wonder some of us don't take the time to celebrate our victories or take the time to think about our accomplishments, to really feel proud of what we've done and what we're good at. You are good at so many things! If you don't believe it, try making a list of the things you're good at or things you've achieved.

Here is an example of some of the things you may have achieved or that you may excel in:

- passed a driving theory test
- graduated high school
- taken a course/classes that you did well in (e.g., cooking class)
- become proficient at a hobby, sport or pastime. (e.g., martial arts grading, showjumping)
- sporting achievements (e.g., making a softball team, cheerleading team)
- volunteering (e.g., riding for the disabled, being on a committee)

- being a good cook, being a good parent, being a good friend, being a good listener
- making your weekly sales or other workplace goals

Now, try to make a similar list of your own. Write down anything that makes you feel proud or that you think you did well. No matter how insignificant it seems, write it down. If it took time and effort, if it made your or someone else's life easier or better, then it is worth celebrating. Keep this list and add to it each day. You'll soon have a list that's very long. If you ever doubt that you're good at anything, take out this list to remind yourself of just how successful you really are!

BE THANKFUL FOR WHAT YOU HAVE

Do you know how lucky you are? It's easy to forget that there are some people in the world who don't have a roof over their heads or who can't be guaranteed a meal every day. Some people live in fear for their lives in warzones. Others are starving. Okay, I said not to compare yourself to others. But there are others who would love to have the things you take for granted every day. Next time you envy someone for having a higher paying job, more money or a bigger house, try to be glad that you are warm, healthy and well-fed. You are lucky. Taking a moment to be thankful will help you put things into perspective.

BE THANKFUL FOR *WHO* YOU HAVE

If you don't feel like you have much in your life to be thankful for, think again. The people who love you are your most precious things of all! People, friends, family, loved ones, beloved pets and kind neighbors, the kind stranger you chat with at the bus stop; all of these people enrich your life. A moment with someone special makes you lucky. If you find yourself comparing yourself to other people who may have more, who may seem more successful or attractive, take a moment to think of what's really important in life. The most important thing in life is the ones you love: if you are loved, liked and cared for then you are rich indeed.

BE AWARE OF MAKING COMPARISONS

It's all very well to try to stop making comparisons, but sometimes we may not even be aware of when we're comparing ourselves to others. Comparisons come so naturally to us that they're ingrained in our behavior. We've been taught to compare ourselves against our peers since we were children. We're literally graded against each other every year until we leave school. So, in order to stop ourselves from comparing ourselves to others, we first need to become more aware of when we're doing so. If we look at someone and wish our skin was smooth like theirs or that we were as friendly or outgoing, the first thing we should do is take note. The next step is to actively stop ourselves from making the comparison. Instead, acknowledge the positive thing about the other person, but don't attach emotion to the feeling. Just accept it and let it go. This is, of course, easier said than done. But with practice, it's possible to acknowledge another person's good qualities without bringing ourselves into the equation.

ACCEPT YOUR FLAWS AND TURN THEM INTO WINS

This may be the most difficult thing to do, but don't think of it as accepting something bad. Flaws can be worked on. Look at them as areas you can improve. For instance, you might think of yourself as being artistically challenged. You might wish you could paint or draw. You might not have done well at art in high school, which forced you to give up on your dream. Instead of giving up for good, why not take drawing classes? With so many classes online, many for free, you don't even need to show anyone your work, at least not straight away. You might not have the best drawing ability naturally, but this will come with time. Maybe you do have a hidden talent in terms of your imagination—you might have a gift for composition or thinking of unique ways to express your subject. If you give up outright, you might never find out how good you can be.

ENJOY THE JOURNEY

Sometimes we can be so focused on our goals that we forget to enjoy the journey on the way. Every step toward your achievement is a success. Every step closer is a win that you should celebrate. If you have just begun to take a journey toward your goal, instead of comparing yourself to someone who seems to be more successful, take the time to appreciate your own efforts. If you look at others and think they are doing better on the same journey, you will lose heart. Don't let this happen. Just focus on what you're doing and think that every small step toward your goal brings you that much closer to what you've been dreaming of.

REPLACE ENVY WITH GETTING TO KNOW PEOPLE

Try not to envy someone who seems better than you. Instead, try to know them. We often see people for what they are instead of who they are. We judge people for their looks, their wealth, their fashion sense. We admire them for their career path and success. We admire someone for being a lawyer or a doctor instead of admiring the person they are. Instead of seeing people as a list of positive traits, we should try to consider their personalities as a whole. When we do this it's easier to realize that, just like us, they aren't perfect. Getting to know someone means seeing the good and bad in them and accepting them. As you get to know the people you may envy, you will see their less perfect sides. The attractive, well-presented person might be lonely or anxious. The successful businessperson might be tired of traveling and jet-setting and wishes they could spend more time with their family. Once you know a person, it's harder to see them as perfect and it's almost impossible to feel jealous of anyone when you know they too have vulnerabilities.

LEARN THAT LIFE ISN'T A COMPETITION

Yes, we've been raised to compete with our peers since we were children. Life can become very stressful if we continue this pattern for the rest of our lives. A bit of healthy competition is good; it can spur you on to do better. You need to know where to draw the line. If competing with others begins to cause you stress, annoyance or jealousy, it may be time to take a step back. Try to concentrate on your own goals instead of looking at how other people are doing. By all means, take advice and learn from other people, especially if they have some good ideas about making tasks easier. But try not to agonize over how much better others are than you. Instead, work on improving yourself in order to make your life better regardless of what others are doing.

CHAPTER SUMMARY

- There are many reasons why comparing yourself to other people in real life or on social media doesn't work. People only tell you the good things about themselves and images on social media are often airbrushed, for instance.

- Comparing yourself doesn't make you do better. In fact, it often makes you do worse for many reasons i.e., comparing can slow your progress.

- There are many things you can do instead of comparing yourself to others. For example, you could focus on your strengths and be thankful for what you have.

In the next chapter, you will learn....

- How self-compassion and taking time for yourself can improve productivity
- Ways to give yourself a break
- Tips for how you can give yourself some "me time" when you're busy

CHAPTER TEN

PRIORITIZE YOUR WELL-BEING

Having a low sense of self-worth can make you feel like you have to make up for your shortcomings by being busy. Taking a break, having fun and nurturing yourself is for those who deserve it. Having low self-worth means you probably don't think you've done enough to deserve time out. Well, guess what, you do deserve it! If you think you don't deserve time out, you're wrong. You do deserve to relax, recharge and unwind.

HOW TIME IMPROVES PRODUCTIVITY

If you find it difficult to slow down and relax because you have so much to do, here's a good reason to put the breaks on: doing too much decreases productivity. According to research,[16] the human brain works to peak performance for one hour at a time. After that, the mind's attention starts to wane. The longer you go without a break after that, the less productive you are. Not taking adequate breaks

---

[16] "For the Most Productive Workday, Science Says ... - Inc. Magazine." 21 Mar. 2019, https://www.inc.com/minda-zetlin/productivity-workday-52-minutes-work-17-minutes-break-travis-bradberry-pomodoro-technique.html. Accessed 12 Jul. 2021.

results in more errors and less productivity. So, if you feel like it's cheating to have a sit-down, think again. By putting your feet up every now and then, you're actually making yourself a better worker!

PRACTICE SELF-COMPASSION

For someone with a low sense of self-worth, one of the things you need the most is to show yourself some love. It is your own negative self-talk that has eaten away your sense of self-worth. So, in order for you to gain self-confidence and grow your sense of worthiness, you need to show yourself some kindness. One of the best ways you can show yourself compassion is to treat yourself the same way as you would a close friend or beloved family member. We are often much kinder to those we care about than we are to ourselves.

After a lifetime of negative self-talk, it may be difficult to know how to treat yourself well. If you find it difficult to treat yourself well, try writing a self-compassion diary. In the diary write down any negative self-talk that you have. As soon as you experience this negative self-talk, debunk it. For instance, if you have failed to lose weight in the past you might have decided that you will be overweight forever. Instead, try to consider other options for weight loss. Some diets don't work for everyone. There's a chance the perfect weight loss program exists for you. There are many options. Instead of thinking you won't ever lose weight, try instead to do some research and try to find a weight loss program that suits you. For instance, some people do well on a fasting diet. Whereas those who need to eat more often and can't go for long periods without eating may be better suited to a calorie restriction diet. Joining a weight loss group with weekly weigh-ins may keep you on track and being in a group of like-minded people who are in the same situation may help spur you on to meet your weight loss goals.

In your self-compassion diary, make notes of your emotions throughout the day. Note when you are feeling stressed. Signs of stress include excessive sweating, a fast heart rate, blushing or reddening, sudden tiredness and jitteriness. As soon as you feel the signs of stress come on try to take a break. Take a few moments in a quiet place to breathe and disconnect. If your workplace doesn't allow a break, acknowledge the feelings you are having and promise yourself you will give yourself a proper break when time allows. If stress in the workplace is overwhelming, talk to your boss or HR about the possibility of minibreaks. Your workplace has an obligation to take care of your mental health needs and they should do what they can to help their workers remain physically and mentally healthy.

TAKING TIME FOR YOURSELF

If you don't take good care of your physical and mental well being you run the risk of burnout. In order to be productive, you need to live a well-rounded life. If all you do is work, you're likely to feel unfulfilled. Feeling like there is nothing to life but work can lead to low mood, lack of motivation and even depression. All of these things inhibit our ability to succeed in life. If all we do is work, we can't ever reach our full potential. The mind needs rest in order to function optimally. In order to think clearly the mind needs time out. In fact, it is often during times of rest that new ideas come to us. When our minds are over-taxed and busy, there is no chance for anything else. During times of rest, inspiration is most likely to strike. When we're stuck on a problem the best chance of reaching a solution is to stop thinking about the task and instead do something enjoyable or relaxing. In order to succeed in life, you need to give your brain the chance to have moments of inspiration.

HOW TO GIVE YOURSELF A BREAK

When you take time out make sure you leave all thoughts of work behind. Try to get away from the place where you work. Your mind needs a complete change of scenery. Going for a walk is a brilliant way to take five. Being in fresh air is invigorating and sunlight will give you a boost of vitamin D, which is essential for your immunity. Sunlight is also essential for your mind. Seasonal Affective Disorder (SAD) occurs during the winter months to some people when they aren't exposed to enough UV light. People can become depressed at this time due to not getting enough sunlight. Symptoms of SAD include feelings of worthlessness, fatigue, sadness and depression. So, getting out in the sun every day is essential to your well-being. If going outside isn't an option, it may pay to use an artificial UV lamp in order to keep SAD at bay, especially if you find yourself feeling less positive during the winter months.

You may feel like you don't have time for hobbies, fun activities or pastimes. Without having an interest outside of work and other obligations you will not experience a balanced life. A balanced life is important for your mood, your happiness and your productivity. There's no point in doing nothing but work if you can't play. If all you do is work, you will soon start to wonder what the point is. Humans need fun time. We're intelligent and curious animals and we need to be stimulated or we can stagnate. Sometimes we may feel unfulfilled because our lives don't have the right balance of work and play. You will be a better employee, parent, partner, friend and human being if you take care of yourself. Having fun is just as important as any other action!

There are many different ways for you to have a break, including a hobby like horseback riding, skiing, sports like softball, swimming, cycling and martial arts. Mixing physical activity with your chosen hobby or pastime is a good way to keep your brain and body in top condition. Physical activity is essential to keep you fit and healthy. It's also good for burning off steam and releasing stress. A pastime that is relaxing is also a good choice if you have a hectic or stressful life. Yoga, Tai Chi and meditation are all wonderful mindfulness practices that will help you release stress and learn to remain calm in everyday life. Try to choose a hobby or sport that interests you. Is there something you've always wanted to try, but that you felt you've never had time for? Now is the time! Perhaps there's something you were good at when you were younger or that you enjoyed as a child. Why not relive your best times and return to an old joy? Remember, don't feel bad about taking time out to do something you love. You are allowed to enjoy yourself. And enjoying yourself will make you more successful. Our minds and bodies are more rested when we relieve stress. Having fun, laughing and having something to look forward to makes us feel good, lifts our mood and gives us a reason to work harder. So don't feel bad, go out and have fun!

TIPS FOR GETTING ME-TIME WHEN YOU'RE BUSY

- Being a parent, especially of young children, will leave you limited alone time. Try going to a gym with a childcare service. You can get fit, burn off energy among adults and your children are supervised, safe and get the chance to socialize. Join a parent's coffee group or walking group. Get to know new people, chat, relax and swap parental stories to give you a boost. Hire a babysitter. It may feel like money wasted, but you can't be a good parent unless you take care of yourself too, and time out is essential in order to cope with the demands of childcare. Ask for help when you need it. You may be upset or annoyed with family members who don't think to offer to help you out. But they don't know you're struggling unless you tell them.

- Instead of driving, or taking a long commute via public transport, walk to work, at least part of the way. You will arrive refreshed and clear-headed and ready to work as well as having burned extra calories. Exercise boosts your mood and increases blood flow making your brain and body ready for a productive day.

- Get to bed early and then rise an hour before you normally would. In that time do something that is refreshing, relaxing or energizing to set yourself up for the day. People who wake up early may be at lower risk of depression and other disorders. They are also more proactive during the day and have a healthier lifestyle with a lower BMI, according to studies.[17] So getting up early and giving yourself some TLC will benefit your life in more ways than one.

- Make yourself the number one priority. Instead of fitting in me-time when you've done everything you can for everyone else, put yourself at the top of the list. Make a commitment to yourself for two or three hours a week. Diary in some indulgent me-time at a spa, have lunch or dinner somewhere nice. If you start treating yourself like you deserve to be spoiled, you will believe you deserve it! Make your special me-time treat a weekly event and set it for the same time. Unless there's an emergency, don't cancel your me-time. It may be hard but learning to say no is one of the best forms of self-care. You don't owe people your time. You can say no. Looking after yourself is the same as any other priority in your life. You don't need to explain yourself when you say no, either. If someone asks why you can't help, just tell them you have an appointment and leave it at that.

- Get help. If you're a parent it's okay to pay for a babysitter in order for you to get not just your work done but also to get a breather for yourself. If you pay someone to look after your children so you can work, take an extra hour for yourself at the end of your working day. Grab yourself a coffee, go for a walk or have a quick drink with some friends. If you work hard in

[17] "5 Health Benefits of Being an Early Riser - Women's Health." 9 Jun. 2014, https://www.womenshealthmag.com/health/a19911162/benefits-of-waking-up-early/. Accessed 12 Jul. 2021.

your day job, household chores can really sap your final energy. If you can afford it, don't feel guilty for paying for someone else to do the gardening or housework. Delegate work to your partner or children. It's good for children to learn responsibility and if you work or need time to yourself, it's okay to ask loved ones to help you out.

CHAPTER SUMMARY

- There are many ways in which taking time out for yourself can improve productivity. For example, not taking enough breaks can actually decrease productivity. The brain will only work to its full potential for an hour at a time.
- There are many ways for you to give yourself some quality time out including taking up a sport or hobby, like Tai Chi.
- There are many tricks to help ensure you get the "me-time" you deserve. For instance, if you're a parent you can try to get some outside help such as hiring a babysitter or a housekeeper.

In the next chapter, you will learn….

- How a good work/life balance will improve all aspects of your life
- How to set boundaries to maintain a balanced life
- How to make good use of time to maintain balance
- How to gain a good life balance by bettering yourself
- How to make balance a priority

CHAPTER ELEVEN

FIND EQUILIBRIUM

If you have a poor work/life balance it means that your working life and your private life are out of equilibrium. Doing extra hours, missing lunch breaks, taking work home with you, taking work calls at home, doing lots of overtime, and even thinking about and planning the next workday in your private time are all signs that you do not have a good work/life balance. Other responsibilities can also disrupt this balance. Parenting and household chores can also put your work/life balance out of equilibrium. Driving your children to extracurricular activities like sports, homeschooling, taking your children to social events, helping with homework, on top of running a household can all make huge demands on your time.

If you don't live a balanced life you can end up burning out. Burning out can lead to a number of problems such as depression, exhaustion, mental breakdown, lowered immunity, recurrent sickness and apathy or boredom. Having a life of pressure and continual stress can lead to a feeling of anxiety and can result in mood disorders like clinical depression.

LEARNING TO SET BOUNDARIES

Setting boundaries at work and in your personal life will help you maintain a balance in your life. Every time your employer asks you to do a little more, you're giving away a part of yourself. Each time you agree to stay at work for another hour you're taking away from your life balance. Set boundaries with your time and energy at work, and stick to them. For instance, make sure you take a full lunch hour. If you have to leave the workplace in order to avoid interruptions then do so. Stick to a manageable workload. It's all very well having set work hours, but if you take on too much work the result can be more stress than if you'd stay late. If too much work is forced upon you by circumstances, remember all you can do is your best. Prioritize the work that needs to be done first, do as much as you can in the time given, but don't feel bad or give extra time or energy to meet unrealistic expectations.

Having boundaries will make people respect your time. The more you give in to requests to take on more work the more often you will be asked to do the same until eventually, people may start to take advantage of you. Being clear from the start about the hours you are able and willing to work, and being clear about the amount of work you can realistically do in a given amount of time will give people clear limits.

Setting boundaries in your private life can be more difficult because you are more emotionally invested in your family. If your children make too many demands of your time in terms of extracurricular activities, ask them to choose which activities they want you to take them to. This will give them an important life lesson—they need to learn they can't always do everything they want to. Organize carpooling with other parents so that you can all share the effort. As soon as they're old enough, teach your children to help with the housework. Giving them real jobs will teach them the importance of having a good work ethic. If you don't have children, get your partner or housemate to help out with the chores. You need to value yourself enough to show people that your time is as important as theirs. If you are spending more time than those you are living with taking care of the house and chores, then you are not giving yourself a good life/work balance.

MAKE GOOD USE OF YOUR TIME

In order to give yourself enough time for the good stuff, you need to ensure that the time at work is well spent. If you find a task is going to be too difficult or is beyond your skills, ask for help, delegate to someone who is more qualified or has the skills to get the task done well and quickly. Ask a co-worker if they can give you advice on how to complete a task if you're unsure. Ask for tips from your boss or co-workers about how you can get tasks done more efficiently. They may well have an idea that cuts down on the time a task takes. In turn, you may also be able to share ways of doing things that make tasks easier. This kind of sharing will not only make your entire workplace more efficient but it will foster good workplace relationships. You won't learn if you don't ask for help and you may keep making mistakes or doing things in a way that takes longer and is less efficient. Be helpful to your co-workers and they may be more inclined to help you as well.

BETTER YOURSELF IN ORDER TO GROW

If all you do is work and if your days are filled with mundane tasks you can start to feel worn down, bored and even apathetic. If even leisure time no longer excites you it may be a sign that you need to stretch your limits. Most jobs are exciting or interesting at first, but when we get used to them they soon become routine and boring. If our days are also filled with mundanity, we can start to stagnate. Aside from going on the occasional holiday, our lives can start to feel meaningless. We all need a higher purpose, a goal to stretch ourselves or a dream to reach for. A good way to bring meaning to your life is to learn something new. Perhaps you could take a night course or learn from home. If you're in a dead-end job, it might be time to further your education to start a more fulfilling career. It's never too late to follow your dreams. Another way to add meaning to your life is to find a way to express yourself. There are many ways to express yourself artistically. You could learn a musical instrument, take up singing, take a creative writing or poetry course. Many people who have reached a point in life where they feel like they have stagnated go on to have a second act. Experiment and try out a few things to find out what you're good at. You never know; you might end up being a famous poet or the next Booker Prize winner. The internet and social media platforms make it easier for people to express themselves. Now more than ever-talented people can reach an audience.

MAKE BALANCE A PRIORITY

Most of our time is spent at work or sleeping. We need to make good use of the time we have left. Balance means meeting a number of needs. Taking care of our bodies is an important part of nurturing ourselves. Trying to make time to have home-cooked, healthy meals is a good way to love yourself. If you eat takeout it may save time in the short term, but your health may be affected. You may not be able to concentrate or sleep well, which will negatively affect your performance in the long run. Fitting in time for physical exercise is equally important. Whether you exercise from home or out in the fresh air, or in a group setting in order to bring your body and mind into balance you should exercise 3–4 times a week. Try to mix up the exercise, don't just walk every day. Also add in some cardio by jogging, doing a spin class or dancing, for instance. If you do a different range of exercises you will ensure you don't get bored and you will be more likely to keep different muscles and parts of your body in good condition.

Once you've taken care of your body, prioritize making sure your mind is taken care of. Sometimes we need to blob out in front of the television in our sweatpants, and if that's what will bring you relaxation and happiness, then don't feel like it's time wasted. Take care not to spend all of your time on devices, however, as this can make you feel like you're wasting your time. Instead, vary what you do during "me-time." Find some fun things to do with other people, in order to fulfill your need for companionship and socializing. Take time outdoors to meet our need to be with nature. Helping others by volunteering or assisting older or disabled neighbors or friends is a good way to pay it forward. Helping others and being selfless will make you feel good about yourself and give your life meaning beyond your own needs. People who help others are known to be happier and more fulfilled in themselves. Remember to nurture your inner child. When we grow up we tend to lose the spark and magic of childhood wonder. Let loose sometimes, run on the beach in bare feet, skip and sing and be carefree and this will help you shed your worries.

In the same way that you dedicate a certain number of hours a week to working, try to set aside time for finding a mind/body balance as well. Once you've found what you enjoy doing, make sure you treat it with as much importance as the less exciting parts of your life. Once your life is in balance; when your health, diet, fitness, social needs, mental health needs, and entertainment needs are met, the difficult parts of your life will be easier to face. Give yourself a lot to look forward to and you will be able to face anything!

CHAPTER SUMMARY

- A good work/life balance will make you more successful in life, whereas working too much and not living a balanced life can have a negative impact. For instance, you may suffer from burnout or anxiety without enough breaks.

- Setting boundaries will allow you to maintain a balanced life. If you give everyone what they ask for all the time you won't have time for yourself. People will respect you and your time more if you set boundaries.

- How making better use of your time will help you achieve balance. For instance, if you get stuck on a task at work, don't just waste time getting nowhere, ask for help.

- Bettering yourself will help you get a life balance. We need to be challenged, but boredom can lead us to feel depressed in our work and our life. Challenge yourself by starting a new course, changing your career, or taking on a new hobby.

In the next chapter, you will learn....

- How rest helps to make you more productive and healthier
- Tips on how to get more rest
- About the importance of sleep

CHAPTER TWELVE

REST AND RECUPERATION

Rest is just as important as exercise and healthy eating for your mental and physical health. Not getting enough rest can be detrimental to our mental health in a number of ways and can be harmful to memory, mood, metabolism and mental health. Not resting can lead to high-stress levels, which has the physical effect of increasing your heart rate, increasing blood sugar levels, and causing stomach issues. Raised sugar levels can lead to prediabetes or diabetes and weight gain. Not getting enough rest can, ironically, disrupt sleep patterns due to the higher level of stress hormones and increased sugar level in your blood. This lack of sleep leads to further physical and emotional problems. Your mood will be affected by a lack of rest. You may end up irritable, easily upset, tearful, and even depressed. If you go without proper rest for long enough you may turn to other ways to relax including alcohol and drug-taking.

You cannot go on without resting indefinitely. You need to give yourself time to recuperate from a busy lifestyle. Without recuperating, we run the risk of suffering the effects of acute stress, which can lead to anxiety, depression, low immunity and susceptibility to illness. About 33% of Americans report[18] feeling stressed and 78% of these claim this stress impacts their health. Resting can reduce the effects of stress or even mitigate them completely. Periodic resting allows the stress hormones associated with working too hard to come down, this, in turn, allows your heart rate to decrease, your blood sugars will return to normal, your memory will improve and your thinking will become clearer. After resting, you will feel refreshed. Productivity at work increases after a period of rest. Recuperation can boost your creativity, making you better at problem-solving. Resting also makes us more resilient to stressful situations. If we suffer from continuous stress our bodies and minds are overwhelmed making us less capable of being able to cope when things go wrong. Conversely, if we've allowed ourselves to recuperate, we're in better physical shape to think clearly and act quickly when we need to.

There are so many positive effects to be had from resting including, improved mood, decreased blood pressure, stronger cardiovascular system, decreased blood sugar, weight loss, improved sleep and better immunity.

HOW TO GET MORE QUALITY REST

Time is the enemy for busy people. Yet, as we've seen if you don't timetable in some "me-time" you'll actually become less productive. Likewise, if you don't get enough rest you will not be as productive,

---

[18] "Why It's Important to Allow Yourself to Rest | INTEGRIS." 16 Apr. 2021, https://integrisok.com/resources/on-your-health/2021/april/why-its-important-to-allow-yourself-to-rest. Accessed 13 Jul. 2021.

WHEN WILL I BE GOOD ENOUGH?

efficient or happy. You must make rest a priority, or your health may suffer.

TIPS TO GET MORE REST

- If you have a job that involves a lot of social interaction with customers and your colleagues, you may benefit from some quiet time to yourself during your breaks. If you can, it may pay to take yourself off to a spare room, sick room, or somewhere peaceful outside where you can sit in complete silence. If your workmates insist on following you, politely excuse yourself and try to find another quiet stop. For a deeper rest, try some breathing exercises, or if you're outside, close your eyes and listen to the sounds around you.

- Listening to music can transport you to another place. Close your eyes and listen to the lyrics. If you're feeling low energy, find a song that will energize you. If you feel a bit frazzled, listen to something relaxing.

- Take a quick walk to a park. A park bench offers a wide range of interesting and calming sights. Seeing children play, watching dogs run around, or seeing people feeding ducks can be relaxing, or just taking in the beauty of your surroundings will help you recuperate.

- Meditation is the closest thing to sleep that you will find. The benefit of meditation is that because you are still conscious, it's a practice that will spill over to your conscious life. If you're having a busy and stressful day, ten minutes of deep meditation can reset your mind, taking you to a level of deep calmness. This calm feeling often stays for a long time once meditation is finished and will help you deal with the stress of the day.

- If you drive to and from work, use this as additional rest time. If you're stuck in traffic, listen to music or an audiobook. There's a reason why many of us feel like nothing more than coming home after a hard day of work and streaming our favorite television show. Human beings are great storytellers. We find stories that transport us to another world. Listening to audiobooks is a good way of relaxing and entertaining ourselves at the same time.

- A good massage is the ultimate relaxation. It may seem a little expensive, but the benefits of massage are significant. Being stressed and busy means we hold a lot of tension in our bodies. Massage is the perfect antidote for the physical effects of stress. A deep tissue massage can be just as relaxing as meditation with the added benefit of physical therapy as well. Choose a massage place that is designed to help you relax, one that has a darkened room and soothing music.

- It may seem like a waste of time, but sometimes streaming your favorite television show is the best kind of relaxation you can have. Having a movie night with family, friends or a loved one makes it an occasion to share with people you care about. Sometimes though, you may just want to curl up in your pajamas and watch something on your own. Indulge yourself by watching your guilty pleasure program. Even though it's not a high-quality drama, sometimes it's good to watch something mindless and silly in order to let your hair down and unwind.

- Reading in bed is one of the most relaxing forms of entertainment. Many people find themselves falling asleep when reading in bed. That's because reading allows you to forget your worries and stresses and it takes you away to another world. Tuck yourself up with a good book and you're guaranteed to feel refreshed afterward.

- Lying out in the sun during a warm day is one of the best forms of rest ever. If you have a comfortable place in your backyard, or on your patio, consider getting a deckchair and having a few moments of sunny recuperation. Pour yourself a nice, cool summery drink with ice. Pretend you're at a high-end resort lounging in the sun. There's no need to pay thousands of dollars to travel to an exotic location when you can pretty much do the same thing in your own backyard!

- Sometimes you may need a whole day of rest. Take the day off work and do nothing. There's something satisfying about sleeping in and spending the day in your dressing gown when all of your colleagues are toiling away without you. You deserve a mental health day every now and then. Just make sure you do the most important thing: nothing!

THE IMPORTANCE OF SLEEP

Getting a good night of sleep is just as important as getting rest throughout the day. During times of stress and when you're busy, it can be difficult to wind down. Even if you fall into an exhausted sleep, the chances are that if you're stressed before you fall asleep you won't have a peaceful rest. You may end up waking often, having nightmares and waking too early without being able to fall back to sleep again. A fitful night's sleep is not a restful one. Falling asleep and continually waking will disrupt your D Sleep, the level of sleep you are in when Rapid Eye Movement (REM(sleep occurs. Taking sleeping aids like sleeping pills and alcohol will not allow you to fall into as deep a sleep as you need to be in order to be fully rested.

A proper night's sleep is essential for your mind and body to function properly. Many essential biological processes happen when we sleep, including:

- the brain incorporates new information and gets rid of unneeded information. Neurons and brain cells are reorganized and toxic byproducts are removed.
- short-term memories are converted to long-term memories
- repairing of cells in the body
- releasing hormones into our bodies for normal functioning
- synthesizes and releases proteins
- tissue growth and repair

The following can occur when you are deprived of sleep:

- mood changes
- poor memory
- poor focus and concentration
- poor motor function
- insulin resistance
- chronic diseases, like diabetes and heart disease
- anxiety
- depression
- fatigue
- weakened immune system
- weight gain
- high blood pressure
- increased risk of early death

As you can see, sleep is important for our minds and bodies to function. Not having enough sleep can have negative consequences. Making sure we get the optimal amount of sleep will help us cope with stress during the day. We cope much better when we have slept properly.

HOW TO GET A BETTER NIGHT'S SLEEP

A good sleep routine is essential for getting enough shut-eye. Start by winding down a few hours before bed. Make sure not to drink coffee too close to bedtime as caffeine will keep you awake. Try to stop using devices a few hours before sleep as the blue light in them can disrupt sleep patterns, or you could try blue-light-blocking glasses. Try to have a calming drink before bed, such as warm milk or chamomile tea. Directly before bed, you could try some calming meditation (we'll show you some good ones to try a little later), or deep breathing. Listening to music with your eyes closed can also help you relax before bedtime. Try not to think of anything that will upset or stimulate you. This can be incredibly difficult as it's often when our mind is quiet that unwanted thoughts intrude. Particularly if you are anxious or under stress, it can be difficult to shut your mind off. A good mindfulness meditation should help because these meditations are designed to quieten the mind. There are some things you can do to help the biological process of falling asleep. Melatonin is the chemical in your brain that controls the circadian rhythm that tells you when it's time to sleep. Going outside during a sunny day in the morning or even opening the curtains in the morning can help regulate your melatonin and set your body clock so that hormones are released at the correct time in order to enable you to sleep. If you have trouble sleeping it may pay to take melatonin in pill form, in order to help this natural process along. Talk to your GP about the benefits of melatonin if you have trouble falling to sleep.

If sleep is a major problem for you it can disrupt your life and cause problems. Talk to your GP about options for helping with sleep. If you find that you aren't refreshed by a full night of sleep, talk to your GP about checking whether there's a physical reason, such as sleep apnea. You could also try getting help with sleep at a sleep clinic. They will monitor your sleep patterns and see if there are behavioral changes you can make to help you catch a few more Zs. There are also some dietary changes you could make to help you ensure a good night of sleep. Such small changes as not drinking caffeine after lunchtime and trying not to eat too late at night may help you fall asleep quicker.

CHAPTER SUMMARY

- Rest can make us more productive and successful because it allows our brains to recharge. This lets us think more clearly and work better.

- There are many ways to squeeze some rest into your busy life including taking a quick walk and going somewhere quiet to meditate.

- Sleep is crucial to our mental and physical health. Sleep helps convert short-term memories into long-term ones and it is during sleep that the body's cells are repaired, for instance.

- Not getting enough sleep can have negative effects on the mind and body. For instance, lack of sleep can result in mood disorders, fatigue, insulin resistance and poor memory.

In the next chapter, you will learn....

- how a positive mindset can challenge negative self-talk and increase self-worth
- about the effects of a positive mindset on your life
- how to achieve a positive mindset

CHAPTER THIRTEEN
THE POWER OF POSITIVITY

A positive mindset is a cure for negative self-talk. A positive mindset isn't about being blindly optimistic. Sometimes it pays to be careful and prepare for the worst. Making the most of things is a way of being positive that will see you through all kinds of situations. If you find yourself struggling with difficult situations like financial hardship, relationship breakdown, illness or bad luck it's hard to be positive, especially if these negative experiences stack up. A positive mindset will allow you to cope with the ups and downs. For instance, if you lose your job it's natural to feel a bit down, but if you have a positive mindset you will be able to pick yourself up and brush yourself off more quickly than if you have a negative mindset. A negative mindset would result in the initial feeling of disappointment about the job loss turning into feelings of blame and unworthiness. Someone with a negative mindset might have such thoughts as, "I'm never going to get another job," or "I'm terrible at any job I get and I'll never do well," or "No one will hire me now." A positive mindset will allow you to take this negative situation and turn it into a positive one. For instance, instead of blaming themselves, someone with a positive mindset will consider the logical reasons for why the negative outcome occurred. They will learn from the negative experience and use it to do better in the future.

A positive mindset means looking at challenges with positivity. For instance, instead of blaming themselves for the job loss, a positively minded person will think of the job loss as beyond their control and they might see it as an opportunity, not a tragedy. Examples of having a positive mindset in this example include positive self-talk like, "This is a great opportunity to try a new career or do further study," or "It's exciting being able to choose a new job, I can be whatever I want!"

Do you see the difference in these two responses? On the one hand, a negative mindset closes down future possibilities and can lead to feelings of worthlessness. On the other hand, the positive mindset leads to feelings of joy in the future and excitement for what comes next. Out of the two examples, which one do you think would be more likely to go on and find a new job? That's right, the positively minded person has more energy and drive to move forward so they are more likely to get a job. The negatively minded person does not feel they're worthy and so they probably won't have as much enthusiasm or self-confidence during the interview process.

Having a positive mindset doesn't just mean thinking well of situations. It also means thinking positively about other people as well. Being able to appreciate the best in others is a powerful ability. Sometimes negative self-talk in ourselves can spill over to our opinion of others. If we don't like ourselves we can blame others for our failures because the negative thoughts we have about ourselves can be too painful to face. For instance, if you didn't manage to pass a test you might feel ashamed and embarrassed causing you to lash out at others. You might blame your teacher or your instructor for your failure. A positive mindset would allow you to see that there are other solutions to help you pass your test the next time. For instance, you could study more, enlist a tutor to help you with your learning or ask for advice on studying from your teacher or tutor.

EFFECTS OF A POSITIVE MINDSET

Research[19] shows there are a number of beneficial outcomes to be had from having a positive mindset.

1. People with a positive mindset report experiencing less stress and they have lower levels of stress hormones adrenaline and cortisol.

2. Positive thinking is proven to increase the immune system and can result in having a longer lifespan.

3. Positive thinkers are far less likely to develop cardiovascular disease.

4. People who think positively tend to do better financially and in their careers.

5. People have better relationships, experience less divorce and stay happily married for longer when they have a positive way of thinking.

---

[19] "How to Create a Positive Mindset and Attitude in Life – Intelligent ...."
https://www.intelligentchange.com/blogs/read/how-to-create-positive-mindset-and-attitude. Accessed 14 Jul. 2021.

HOW TO GAIN A POSITIVE MINDSET

Having a low sense of self-worth is driven by negative self-talk. Negative self-talk becomes so ingrained that we aren't even aware of it. To some extent negative self-talk occurs on a subconscious level; it's deep-rooted and difficult to change. But a few simple exercises and behaviors can turn negative self-talk into positive thinking. Using the following exercises won't just make you happier, they'll change your thought patterns into positive ones that will help you thrive and succeed.

1. Write a thankfulness journal. In your thankfulness journal write something you're thankful for each day. It needn't be anything large. Write about being thankful that the sun is shining on a cool winter day. Write about how lucky you are to have a sibling that you get along well with. Write about how a customer made you feel good about yourself when they thanked you for doing so much for them. Write about your kind neighbor who lifted your spirits when they complimented what you were wearing. The more you write in the journal the more you will realize how much you have to be thankful for. You will probably find that you get better at noting what's good in the world around you. You'll probably end up filling pages in just one day! Don't hold back, learn to see how lucky you are each day and you will find yourself feeling more positive about the small things. If you find your positive mindset slipping, just take out your thankfulness journal to see how much there is for you to be thankful for. Don't feel like

anything you write is silly or not worth noting—happiness is a state of mind. No one else will see your diary. There are no right or wrong answers. If something makes you smile, or gives you a boost, put it in your diary. The more you can find to be thankful for, the happier you will be!

2. Change your thinking about rejection or failure. It's hard to put a positive spin on rejection or failure. You don't have to pretend these experiences aren't upsetting. Once you've acknowledged your feelings, try to turn them into a positive. Seeing failures as a chance to learn or grow is a way of turning a bad thing into something you can think of as a way of making a better future for yourself. The first step in learning from failure or rejection is to analyze it. Try to figure out why the outcome occurred without judging yourself and see if there's anything you can do differently next time. For instance, if you fail to land a job after an interview, try to figure out if you could have answered the questions any differently. Look at your skills, qualifications and past work experience. Are they what the job needed? If it seems like there's nothing you could do differently, try to understand that you weren't the only candidate going for the job. Perhaps the other candidates were more highly qualified. Perhaps they have more experience on the job than you do. This is where analysis comes in handy. Instead of blaming yourself, try to think about why it wasn't your fault that you didn't get the job. Failure is the first step toward success. Many billionaires, famous or successful people have failed. In fact, it's not success that promises a person a

bright future—it's tenacity and the ability to keep on trying. With every failure, learn. With every rejection, grow. If you fail an exam, it's not because you're stupid. Maybe you didn't study hard enough. Maybe you need tuition. Whatever the case, you can go back, re-sit the exam and succeed!

3. Use positive affirmations. Positive affirmations are positive statements about yourself or a given situation that debunk your negative self-talk. By making positive statements over and over you can retrain your brain to think positively. This will put an end to your negative self-talk by replacing these thoughts with positive ones. Positive affirmations go beyond just curing us of negative self-talk. Positive affirmations can improve your performance in all areas of life. Studies[20] show that positive affirmations can help increase self-esteem, increase your willpower (for instance, increased likelihood of sticking to a diet and exercising), decrease stress, and increase performance at work and college. To make a positive affirmation write down some of the aspects of your life that you'd like to change. Write an affirmation in the present tense. For instance, if you want to feel confident giving a speech at a wedding your positive affirmation could go something like this, "I am able to speak clearly, my speech is well-rehearsed and I know it off by heart. I will speak with confidence and humor." In order to make your affirmation work best, try to use emotion when you rehearse the affirmation. For instance, if you're concerned

---

[20] "Positive Psychology: Positive Daily Affirmations: Is There Science ...." 16 Mar. 2021, https://positivepsychology.com/daily-affirmations/. Accessed 23 Jul. 2021.

about starting a new hobby that will put you out of your comfort zone, tell yourself, "I look forward to trying new things and I'm excited about this challenge!"

CHAPTER SUMMARY

- A positive mindset will put an end to negative self-talk and help you to face the challenges of daily life. Instead of seeing the negative in challenging situations, a positive mindset helps you to see opportunities and seek out solutions.
- There are many positive effects of having a positive mindset. For instance, being positive can increase immune system functioning and decrease stress.
- There are a number of ways to gain a positive mindset. For instance, keeping a thankfulness journal and using positive affirmations.

In the next chapter, you will learn....

- about the tools you've been given to help you to answer the question: When Will I Be Good Enough?
- to revisit the things that can help you feel like you are good enough.

CHAPTER FOURTEEN

I AM GOOD ENOUGH

The most essential question remains: Am I good enough? This is a question that all humans begin to ask themselves from the minute they learn how to color inside the lines. And yet, no matter how much we try, none of us can escape this persistent nagging that we are not good enough. *Am I a good enough father? Am I good enough to win this contract? Am I a good enough wife? Am I a good enough doctor? Am I a good enough student?* The questions never seem to leave us.

Wanting to finally know or hear that we are good enough, many of us try different methods to rid ourselves of the shame of our insecurities but the consumerist world in which we live feeds our self-doubt. Our hair is not as shiny as it should be. Our presents are not expensive enough to scream, "I love you" to our loved ones. And our car will never be the most advanced model. Today, more than ever it seems, with modern consumerism heightened by the advent of social media, our confidence is tested on a daily basis and our anxiety levels are raised through the roof.

Despite its quasi-unsolvable nature, shame is now part of everyday human interaction. Public shaming is now a commonplace occurrence, found on all social media sites, where people shame both random individuals in public and close acquaintances. Worse still, in extreme reaction to an extremely individualistic environment, there is now a narcissism epidemic spreading across the world, according to psychologists Jean Twenge and W. Keith Campbell in their book, *The Narcissism Epidemic*.[21] We are all so desperate to be good enough that we are moving too close to the other side of inferiority: superiority. To live a happy, healthy life, you will have to find a happy medium: healthy self-esteem. Hence, when you ask, "Am I good enough?" what you really want to ask is: "Do I have intrinsic worth?" In human societies, both past and present, humans have rarely been awarded intrinsic worth. We have to work and struggle to finally be considered temporarily worthy after every achievement. The local man who builds a successful dentist practice is worthy until his practice suddenly begins to fail. The student at school with the highest grade is celebrated until her grades begin to slip. Our world is not built to offer others intrinsic worth.

And yet, the truth remains and will always remain that every human being is intrinsically worthy. There is nothing that can make you, or anybody else, any more or less worthy. The simple truth, whether you believe it or not, is that you *are* worthy. What is more important is learning to see and believe this truth.

Of course, this is easier said than done. From childhood, we are consistently judged. Sometimes we are considered worthy and other

---

[21] Twenge, J.M. & Campbell, W.K. (2010, April 13). *The Narcissism Epidemic: Living In The Age Of Entitlement*. Atria Books.

WHEN WILL I BE GOOD ENOUGH?

times we are not. We learn to chase after the feelings of contentment and worthiness during those times when we succeed. We act like addicts, chasing a high that is only temporary and will never fulfill us. Your car, no matter how expensive, will serve as a constant reminder that there are more expensive cars that more financially successful people can afford. We might be beautiful, but there will always be someone more beautiful. Unfortunately, humanity is fickle. Whoever is more successful, more beautiful, more intelligent and so on, is praised. But when someone even more successful, more beautiful or more intelligent appears, we are discarded cruelly out of the warm embrace of their spotlight. Your father might praise you for your academic successes, but does he simply tell you that he loves you for who you are? In the former, you must always succeed to be loved; therefore, you naturally start out as being unworthy. In the latter, you are loved and so you feel more confident to pursue life and to succeed, therefore you are intrinsically valuable.

To be human is to have a need to hear that you are good enough. Psychologist Abraham Maslow, in his famous theory of the hierarchy of human needs[22], classified this as "self-esteem." While not a basic need, self-esteem is our need for respect and confidence that must be met if we are to reach our full human potential. Without it, who we are is lost to mood disorders, mental illnesses and even personality disorders.

---

[22] McLeod, S. (2018, May 21). *Maslow's Hierarchy Of Human Needs*. Canada College. https://canadacollege.edu/dreamers/docs/Maslows-Hierarchy-of-Needs.pdf.

While fulfilling basic human needs will keep us alive, our lives remain miserable if we do not fulfill our need for esteem. We know that personal trauma, past experiences and society's ravenous demands for success are keeping you from seeing your true reflection as a swan rather than as an ugly duckling.

Until you find that voice within that screams, "YES!, I am good enough!" you will never silence the voice that lies to you, telling you that you are not good enough. This is where self-compassion comes in. Self-compassion, as we have covered in previous chapters, is loving yourself through your words, thoughts and actions. Self-compassion is treating yourself with the respect and the care that a person with intrinsic worth deserves. It is not tied to how well your stocks did or how expensive your possessions are. Self-compassion mandates that you deserve to be treated with the utmost care, kindness and love. Instead of waiting for others to voice that you are good enough, self-compassion takes the initiative and steps up to answer that querying voice.

"YES! I am good enough!"

These are the most important words that you can utter to yourself. They are a positive affirmation and a mantra rolled into one super force. They are words that go to the deepest wounds and most traumatic moments of your life, bringing healing with them. They are words that will help you to stand tall when others tell you you are not good enough or treat you like you are worthless. They are like the fertilizer for the seed of your self-esteem, giving you the strength to finally see yourself for who you are.

WHEN WILL I BE GOOD ENOUGH?

"YES! I am good enough!"

Remember that these positive affirmations do not have to come from your mouth alone. Self-affirmations are incredibly important. Without them, we would never believe when others affirm us. If an ugly duckling refuses to believe that he is a swan, then his self-image would never change, no matter what the other swans around him said to try to change his mind. Similarly, you must allow yourself to believe your self-affirmations. You must remember that while it is tempting to wait for others to tell you who you are, the real power comes from within. You are responsible for yourself and you are responsible for your self-esteem. The hint is in the word SELF-esteem.

Whilst we are responsible for our esteem, we should acknowledge the desire inside us all to be validated by others. Repressing this need is not enough; you must nurture it the right way. Surround yourself with people who truly love you. People who truly love you will naturally affirm you because they care about you. When you feel down, they will lift you up and even carry you through tougher times. They won't lie or overstate your worth. They will be truthful towards you, reflecting a real image of yourself back to you. When you surround yourself with people who love and care for you, you surround yourself with people whose love calls you good enough, even during times when you may doubt yourself.

Finally, don't discount the use of therapy. If you find that the voice calling you not good enough becomes loud and persistent, therapy is another form of self-compassion. Therapy is a great way to dig through the traumatic roots of your anxieties or insecurities and start to rebuild your mental resilience and self-belief.

CHAPTER SUMMARY

- Every human being is intrinsically worthy.
- To be human is to have a need to hear that you are good enough.
- We can not fulfill our potential if we do not fulfill our need for esteem.
- Self-compassion involves surrounding yourself with people who love you and affirm your worth.
- YES! You are good enough!

In the next chapter, you will learn....

- 10 Mindfulness meditations to help you relax and enable you to think clearly

CHAPTER FIFTEEN

10 MINDFULNESS MEDITATIONS

Mindfulness meditations teach us how to "be in the moment." Our busy lives mean we're always on the go, running around trying to get everything done at once. Our thoughts are likewise going at a hundred miles an hour. Negative self-talk can fill our minds with thoughts we don't want to listen to and when we're under stress it's harder to block negative thoughts out. Mindfulness meditations can teach us how to live for right now. With mindfulness, we can put aside negative thoughts, stress and worry. Meditation is one of the best things you can do to relax. So sit, or lie back, close your eyes and prepare to relax with 10 mindfulness meditations.

1. Spiritual meditation: This meditation takes you away from the worries of this world by connecting you to your god or the universe. During this meditation, lie down or sit comfortably. Close your eyes and try to relax. As you lay there, try to allow the quietness around you to relax you further. Once you feel relaxed contemplate your god or think about the universe. When thinking of your god, consider how thankful you are for them and how much you love them. If you would prefer to

think about the universe, try contemplating the vastness of space and how every atom is connected and that you are a part of an eternal, everlasting system. You can try essential oils to increase the spirituality of the experience. For instance, frankincense and sage can be used. This meditation will be helpful if you are seeking a higher purpose or wanting to experience something larger than yourself. By feeling a connection to something beyond you and your worldly concerns you can relax, gain perspective and feel part of something wonderful.

2. Movement Meditation: Tai Chi is one way to mix movement with mindfulness. It is also possible to turn any kind of movement into a form of mindfulness meditation. Try a walking meditation by beginning your walk very slowly. Notice how your heels touch the ground followed by your toes. Notice how your feet feel as you lift them. Move up your body, being aware of how your arms move. Speed up and feel how each part of your foot changes with the motion and how your arms move more quickly. If you feel yourself losing mindfulness, slow down again. This mindfulness meditation is ideal for those who don't like sitting still and find they are most relaxing when doing something physical.

3. Buddhist mindfulness meditation: In this meditation begin as always by making sure you are relaxed. Close your eyes and pay attention to the first thought that comes into your head. Don't judge the thought, or contemplate it too deeply. Instead, you should take note of the thought without becoming too

involved in it. You may also take note of other sensations, like the sounds you hear or the temperature of the room, in the same way. Continue to observe thoughts, sensations and feelings that you experience. This meditation is an excellent mindfulness technique to use if you find yourself being reactive to the things going on in your life. Here you can learn to observe things without reacting too strongly to them.

4. Transcendental meditation: To begin this meditation, find your comfortable position, close your eyes and relax. At the same time use a mantra of your choice; for instance, the word "om" is traditionally used. The mantra is repeated over and over. Some people will use a word or even a phrase. The mantra is generally not repeated aloud. Don't try to push the phrase onto your mind. Don't try to connect with the mantra too forcefully. Just repeat the mantra over and over calmly while continuing to go into a deeper state of relaxation. Your mind may wander and other thoughts or sensations may come to you or distract you. Don't panic or be upset if this happens. It's perfectly natural. Just try to bring yourself back to the mantra. It's possible this type of mindfulness meditation is so successful because it creates almost a trancelike state somewhere between sleep and wakefulness.

5. Loving-Kindness meditation: This is a very positive kind of meditation. To begin, relax, close your eyes and draw the kindness of the universe into you. Now send the kindness and love outward to the people you love, to the people you don't know who need it, and most of all to those people who have

wronged you. If you can do the latter you have shown incredible emotional growth and forgiveness. If you yourself feel hurt, angry or upset by something someone has done to you, then this is an incredibly healing form of meditation. You needn't wish kindness to those who have hurt you if you aren't ready for that yet, but wishing love to others is a way for you to feel in control of negative outcomes in the world. It will also make you feel good about yourself and boost your own sense of self-worth. Doing this will let you know you are a good person and that you want to help others.

6. Focussed meditation: This meditation involves focussing on one thing. The focal point can come from any of the senses. For instance, you could focus on your breathing, or you could focus on the sounds coming from outside your window. You could focus on a repetitive sound like a gong, stare at a flame or count mandala beads. If you find it hard to focus or have difficulty in keeping your mind from wandering, this meditation may be ideal due to the fact that you have a tangible focal point to concentrate on.

7. Body scan meditation. This meditation uses the physical sensation of tightening and then releasing muscles to create a sense of release and ultimately bring about relaxation. If you hold onto a lot of physical tension this meditation may be ideal because it will teach you how to release the tension you are holding. Start with your toes and squeeze for a few seconds and then release, noticing any sensations felt before and after you have released. Move onto your entire foot, up the ankle,

the leg, the knee all the way up to the top of the head, squeezing and releasing as you go. This meditation is especially good if you are a person who is physical.

8. Zen meditation. Rather than focussing on an object, a sensation or thought, this meditation is about posture. To do this meditation you will need to sit in the lotus position. To achieve the lotus position, begin by crossing your legs. Then place your right foot on your left thigh and place your left foot on your right thigh so that the underside of your foot is facing upward. As this position may be difficult, you may like to begin by crossing your legs or sitting up straight in a chair. Place your hands in the cosmic mudra position. With your palm up, place your right hand on your left foot. Do the same with your left hand but on the right foot. The tips of the thumbs should touch slightly. Sit still and concentrate on keeping a good posture with your shoulders but relaxed. Merely staying in this posture, remembering to relax and not slouch will place you in a meditative state. This meditation is good for those who may have posture issues. Learning to have a good posture in a meditative state will help you keep a good posture in everyday life. This may be difficult if you have body pains or injuries.

9. Taoist meditation: This meditation had three phases. Firstly, begin by concentrating on something. This is known as the first adjustment. The second adjustment involves becoming more relaxed in your body. The energy you have put into concentrating on the first adjustment should help you to relax

your body. The third adjustment is to ensure that your breathing becomes slow, even and soft. Each of these phases is meant to bring your mind and body into harmony. This makes sense because as you relax your body, your breathing will relax and then your mind will follow. This is a good meditation if it takes you a while to relax. Having a few separate phases allows you to try different methods in order to relax more deeply. If you find your mind is too busy and meditation makes you feel hyperactive or agitated, this meditation may help you by making the body relax first.

10. Qigong: This ancient Chinese meditation utilizes the body's energy. In this meditation, use is made of energy in your body to heal yourself or sending healing outward. To begin this meditation visualize the energy in your body. Think about moving energy through pathways, opening and closing them and allowing energy to pass through. Sending energy inward through these pathways or "meridians" is said to heal yourself. Sending energy outward is thought to heal others. If you are anxious, upset, or angry the act of channeling energy to your mind may help to calm you more effectively than meditation that concentrates purely on relaxation. The intent of healing can have a positive effect on the mind and body.

If one of two of these kinds of meditation captures your interest, try them out. You may need to try most or all of these to figure out which one suits you best. You could also try different types of meditation for different reasons or to suit different moods.

FINAL WORDS

Overcoming feelings of low self-worth and figuring out how to find happiness again are complex, tricky issues that take time. With this book as your guide, you should feel more comfortable in the belief that your feelings about not being good enough have nothing to do with whether or not you're a worthy person. You are a worthy person. You are good enough.

You now understand the many pitfalls to avoid in order to stop feeding those feelings of low self-worth and you have gained a plethora of strategies to help you live your life with a greater degree of confidence and resilience than before. You have the tools to invalidate your negative inner voice and you have learned how to gain perspective. You understand how to apply logic to critically and objectively assess and validate situations and use it to kick negativity to the curb. These are powerful tools which will help you to feel more content and lead you on your path to happiness.

By cultivating positive lifestyle habits you open the doors of opportunity to provide a brighter future, enriched with interest and excitement, to spark passion and put fire in your belly. Positive affirmations and mindfulness meditations will help you to live in the moment and find peace and tranquility in order to avoid feeling overwhelmed in today's fast-paced and often chaotic world.

Learning to practice guilt-free self-compassion gives you a herculean antidote to tackling feelings of low self-esteem and has the power to breed success across all areas of your life. If you can prioritize self-compassion, you will thrive on its endorphins and find the happiness you seek.

You now know the truth, that you *are* good enough and you know how to nurture your self-worth and grow in confidence to find happiness again.

Repeat after me: **I *am* worthy; I *am* good enough.**